From Your Friends At The MAILBOX® Magazine

FEBRUARY

A MONTH OF IDEAS AT YOUR FINGERTIPS!

PRESCHOOL–KINDERGARTEN

WRITTEN BY

Barbara Backer, Jan Brennan, Diane Gilliam, Linda Gordetsky, Ada Hanley Goren, Lucia Kemp Henry, Angie Kutzer, Carrie Lacher, Suzanne Moore, Mackie Rhodes, Karen P. Shelton

EDITED BY

Lynn Bemer Coble, Ada Hanley Goren, Mackie Rhodes, Jennifer Rudisill, Karen P. Shelton, Gina Sutphin

ILLUSTRATED BY

Marilynn G. Barr, Jennifer T. Bennett, Cathy Spangler Bruce, Pam Crane, Teresa Davidson, Clevell Harris, Susan Hodnett, Sheila Krill, Rob Mayworth, Rebecca Saunders, Barry Slate, Donna K. Teal

TYPESET BY

David Jarrell
Lynette Maxwell

COVER DESIGNED BY

Jennifer T. Bennett

Be Mine!

TABLE OF CONTENTS

February Calendar

Responsible Pet Owner Month

Owning a pet is wonderful, but it's also a big responsibility. Spend the month discussing the important aspects of pet care with your children. Invite a veterinarian to visit and to emphasize good pet owner habits. Your little ones might also benefit from pet-handling instructions and safety tips regarding stray animals. With parents' help, schedule visits from your children's pets throughout the month. Children will enjoy sharing their pets and how they help take care of the pets. No pet at home? No problem! Stuffed animals or animal pictures will work for children to show a pet they would like to have. This "purr-ade" of pampered pets is sure to please!

National Wild Bird–Feeding Month

Encourage your little ones to help the birds over the hardships of winter by providing some nourishment. There are lots of easy ways to feed our feathered friends. Spread pinecones or bagels with peanut butter; then roll them in sunflower seeds. String several different types of cereal, or collect and crumble uneaten bread before lunches are thrown away. Distribute the treats on trees, on bushes, or on the ground in front of your windows. Your children's beaks will be glued to the glass as they observe the many kinds of birds that will be flying by to feast!

5—The Wiffle® Ball Was First Sold

Celebrate the Wiffle® ball! Use this unique ball for several activities today. Toss it to a child when it's her turn to answer any question, and she'll toss it back to you when she finishes. List students' estimations of how many holes a Wiffle® ball has and then count the holes to see who came close. Make a class collage of pictures of other things that have holes. Explain that the Wiffle® ball has holes in order to lessen the distance it will travel. The holes allow air inside the plastic, which helps slow the ball down. During free time, have several Wiffle® balls and rubber balls available so that students can explore this phenomenon.

7—Birthdate Of Laura Ingalls Wilder

The author of the popular series of Little House books was born on this day in 1867. Laura Ingalls Wilder wrote nine books based on her recollections of life on the American frontier. Share one of the winter stories—*Dance At Grandpa's* or *Winter Days In The Big Woods* from the series My First Little House Books (Scholastic Inc.)—with your children while they sip some warm cider. Your little ones can also make their own frost pictures—like Laura did—on the classroom door and windows.

11—Birthdate Of Thomas Edison

Thomas Edison is considered to be one of America's most influential inventors. His development of practical lighting and more than 1,200 patents made him an integral part of his society and of future generations. Since Edison and his lightbulb are synonymous with bright ideas, help your children pay homage to Edison. Have them finger-paint—with yellow paint—a small piece of white paper. Make a lightbulb pattern for them to trace on their painting (when it's dry). Have your students cut out their lightbulbs and color the bottom tips of the bulbs black. Attach the bulbs to sentence strips and staple the strips to fit your children's heads. They will love putting on their thinking caps to celebrate the spirit of invention.

14—Read To Your Child Day

We all know how important listening to literature is to little ones. Read To Your Child Day is a perfect time to encourage this reading. Announce this special day a week ahead of time, and ask parent volunteers to come in and read to your children. Schedule a 20-minute storytime for each parent, with breaks in between for movement. At the end of the day, send a book home with every child in your class. On the cover, attach (so that it can easily be removed) a short note explaining the special day and asking the parent to share the story with the child and return the book the next day. Who knows—this might spark a nightly routine of reading if one hasn't been established already!

20—Hoodie Hoo Day

Only one more month of winter! If the doldrums of winter have taken over your classroom, get rid of them today! Take your children outside and do what some people in the Northern Hemisphere do—shout, "Hoodie Hoo!" several times to chase winter away. Afterwards bring your children back inside, and have them draw pictures of warmer and brighter days.

26—Birthdate Of Levi Strauss

Jeans have been a popular addition to the wardrobe since their creation, so why not celebrate the man who made the world's first pair? Invite everyone to wear jeans, or something made of denim, today. Share a collection of denim items and brainstorm with your students other things that are made from denim. Use this list as headings as you make a graph to show how many children have each of these items. Give each child a rectangle of denim material. Supply an assortment of fabric paints and let your little ones decorate the denim to make placemats. Use these placemats at snacktime when your children munch on cupcakes honoring Levi's birthday.

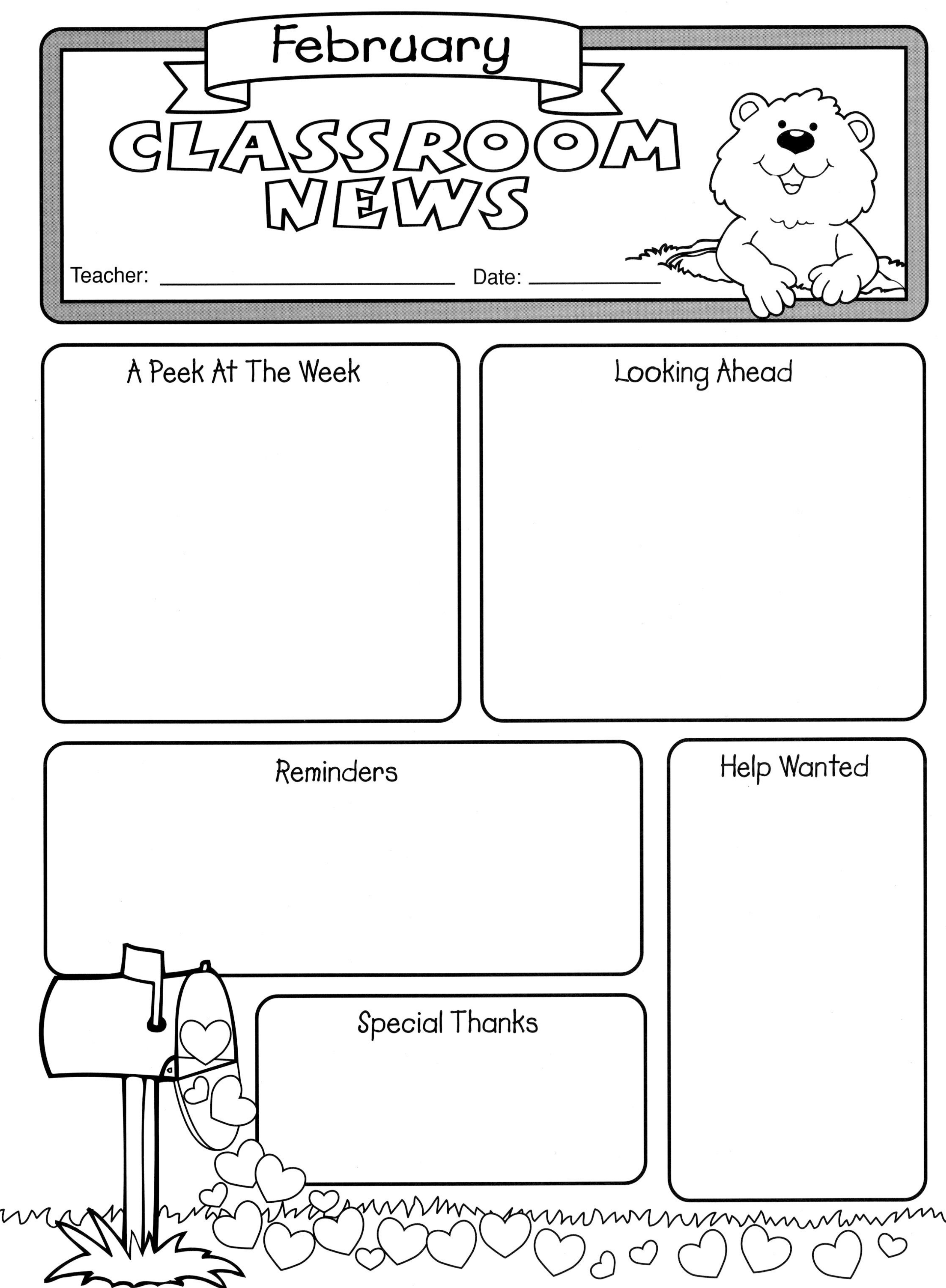
February
CLASSROOM
NEWS
Teacher:
Date:
A Peek At The Week
Looking Ahead
Reminders
Help Wanted
Special Thanks

TIP-TOP TEETH

If National Children's Dental Health Month has you searching for ideas your students can sink their teeth into, try this multidisciplinary unit. Begin with a grand entrance and a song-and-dance routine, and soon your little ones will be anxious to spruce up their pearly whites.

ideas contributed by Linda Gordetsky

Happy Smiles Brush Through Here!

Happy Smiles Brush Through Here!

Greet your students with a giant toothbrush door decoration to announce your dental health studies. For bristles, cut white plastic garbage bags into strips and tape them to the top of your classroom door frame. Cut out bulletin-board paper to complete a giant toothbrush. Program it with a dental health slogan. Each morning, students will enjoy "brushing" through the doorway, and you'll be sure to see happy smiles as they do!

Brushing Up!

Tape-record your class singing the following tune. While you play the tape, assist your children in forming a circle and choosing motions that correspond to each line of the song. When you come to the chorus each time, do the usual "Hokey-Pokey" moves.

Brushy, Brushy

(sung to the tune of "The Hokey-Pokey")

You put your toothpaste on.
Watch it squeeze right out.
Put your toothpaste on,
And squish it all about.

Chorus:
You do the Brushy, Brushy,
And you move it all around.
That's what it's all about.
Brushy, Brushy!

You put your toothbrush in.
Don't take your toothbrush out.
You put your toothbrush in,
And you scrub it all about.

Chorus:
You do the Brushy, Brushy,
And you move it all around.
That's what it's all about.
Brushy, Brushy!

Now put some water in.
Don't let the water out.
Now put some water in,
And swish it all about.

Chorus:
You do the Brushy, Brushy,
And you move it all around.
That's what it's all about.
Rinse out!

Checkup

Before beginning this exploration activity, have each youngster wash his hands thoroughly. Provide a metal or Mylar® mirror for each child in your group. Direct students to open wide and take a peek at their teeth. Guide them in discussing and discovering things about their teeth by asking a series of questions. For example, you might ask students what color their teeth are, how many there are, and whether any teeth are loose or missing. You might also discuss the body parts that are adjacent to the teeth, such as the gums, lips, and tongue. As your discussion progresses, write what students know about teeth on an experience chart.

Fabulous Foods

Introduce your youngsters to the facts that some foods are helpful to teeth and some foods can be harmful. Explain that some foods can be beneficial because they can actually help clean the surfaces of teeth and because they can give the body necessary nutrients to promote the growth of strong, healthy teeth. Give some examples, such as milk, apples, and cheese. Then ask students to name other foods that might be good for teeth.

Then provide students with magazines and safety scissors, and ask them to cut out pictures of all kinds of foods. When all your students have contributed to the collection, hold up one picture at a time and ask students to comment on whether the food shown is primarily beneficial or harmful to teeth. Without explaining what you are doing, attach each picture to a piece of chart paper that has been divided into two columns so that all the healthful foods are on one side and all the harmful ones are on the other. When you have attached all the pictures, ask students what they notice about each column of pictures. Title each column as the children suggest.

Mr. Big Mouth

Mr. Big Mouth can be an invaluable tool in teaching about dental health. To make Mr. Big Mouth, tape shut the flaps of a sturdy cardboard box. Flip the box upside down; then paint two eyes and a mouth on it as shown, taking care to leave at least enough of an opening in the mouth so that a child's arm will fit through it. Cut away the opening between the upper and lower teeth. Cut narrow channels between the teeth, so that real floss or string will fit between them.

Each day during your dental health studies, put a different array of foods in a basket before the children arrive. Some should be foods that are good for the teeth and some foods that are not. Have children take turns choosing a food from the basket. If he has pulled out a food that is beneficial for teeth, have him "feed" it to Mr. Big Mouth. If the food is not good for teeth, have him continue pulling items from the basket until a healthful alternative is selected. See "Floss And Brush" on page 9 for another way to use Mr. Big Mouth.

Our Friend The Dentist

The Berenstain Bears Visit The Dentist by Stan & Jan Berenstain (Random House, Inc.) is a delightful complement to your dental health studies. (*Just Going To The Dentist* by Mercer Mayer [Western Publishing Company, Inc.] is also a good choice for introducing this activity.) Read the story aloud—paraphrasing for younger children if necessary. Follow up the story with a discussion about dental care workers, emphasizing the concept that a dentist helps keep our teeth strong and healthy. Also explain that when our teeth are in need of repairs, the dentist can take care of that too.

If desired, use the patterns on page 15 to create a headband for the dentist, one with flowers for the mother, and one with a cap's bill for the child in the song below. After students have learned the song, have them wear the appropriate headbands and act out the drama described in the song. Repeat this activity until every child has had a turn to play a role.

There's Nothing Like Being There!

Give students an opportunity to visit a local dentist's office and talk to the personnel there. You may even stage the entire trip as an appointment for a doll or stuffed animal that has a particularly toothy grin. If you choose this alternative, the children could check the patient in at the front desk and seat him in the dentist's chair when they enter the examination room. The dentist may even pretend to give the patient's teeth a quick exam. Regardless of whether a mock patient is involved or not, photograph the students during their field trip. Back in your classroom, share with students a factual book, such as *When I See My Dentist...* by Susan Kuklin (Bradbury Press) or *My Dentist* by Harlow Rockwell (Greenwillow Books). Give students opportunities to tell which scenes from the book remind them of things they saw at the dentist's office.

Ouch, My Tooth!

(sung to the tune of "There's A Hole In The Bucket")

My tooth hurts, dear Mama, dear Mama, dear Mama.
My tooth hurts, dear Mama. I must say it hurts.

We'll go to the dentist, dear Tommy, dear Tommy.
We'll go to the dentist. I'll call her right now.

She sees a small hole in one bright shiny tooth.
She sees a small hole in one bright shiny tooth.

Oh, how did it get there, dear Dentist, dear Dentist?
Oh, how did it get there—that hole in my tooth?

You ate too much candy and cookies and soda.
You ate too much sugar—and needed to brush.

You made it feel better, dear Dentist, dear Dentist.
You made it feel better. I promise to brush!

My, What A Toothy Grin!

Read aloud Taro Gomi's *The Crocodile And The Dentist* (Scholastic Inc.). When the giggles subside, have students use context clues to complete the following sentences: "Once there was a little ___ who woke up with a toothache. His mother called the ___ who said, 'You may have a ___. You must ___ more often and stop eating so much ___.' " Then let student volunteers take turns saying something related to teeth, but omitting words for their classmates to supply.

> "Brush them and floss them and take them to the dentist, and they will stay with you. Ignore them and they'll go away."
> —American Dental Association

Floss And Brush

Prepare Mr. Big Mouth (see page 7) for this activity by stuffing some green and brown tissue-paper pieces between some of his teeth. Read students the quote shown from the American Dental Association. Find out what your children think that it means. Turn their attention to Mr. Big Mouth's teeth. Ask them to comment on what they see. What would they suggest to do to care for these yucky teeth?

Using string, demonstrate proper flossing methods—using a gentle up-and-down motion to rub the sides of Mr. Big Mouth's teeth. Explain that flossing precedes brushing and that children should always have parental assistance when flossing their own teeth. Choose a child to wear the dentist headband (see "Our Friend The Dentist" on page 8), and help him floss Mr. Big Mouth's teeth with string to remove the buildup between his teeth. Then replace the tissue-paper pieces and have the dentist choose another student to take a turn wearing the dentist's headband and flossing Mr. Big Mouth's teeth. After giving several children a turn, show students what real dental floss looks like and explain that imitation floss was used to floss Mr. Big Mouth's teeth.

Explain to students that after teeth are flossed, they must be brushed. Using short, *gentle* strokes, brush the fronts and backs of Mr. Big Mouth's teeth. Scrub gently on chewing surfaces. Give students who have not yet had an opportunity to care for Mr. Big Mouth's teeth a turn to brush his pearly whites.

Tempting Tooth Tales

Tempt parents to join in reading some dental delights by providing a list of related children's books. Duplicate the toothbrush bookmark pattern on page 12. Assist each child in cutting out her copy of the pattern; then assist her in folding the paper so that the writing is folded to the inside, using the partial dotted lines as guides. Show each student how to fringe the widest part of her cutout to resemble the bristles on a toothbrush. Provide art supplies so that each student can decorate the handle of her toothbrush with her favorite colors. Encourage each child to show her toothbrush to her parents and read some tooth tales with them also.

My Tooth Is Loose
by
Ms. Gordetsky's Class

Wouldn't it be awful if your tooth fell out while you were on a wild ride!

Crunchin'

During your dental health unit, supplement your students' lunches by bringing in some crunchy foods for students to try. Include an assortment of fresh vegetables and fruits. Before having lunch, say the following rhyme with your students; then encourage them to try several of the crunchy foods that you have provided along with their lunches. After lunch, ask your children to name the crunchy and noncrunchy foods they tried. Then encourage them to describe the crunchy foods. Repeat the rhyme again to drive home the message that crunchy fruits and vegetables are helpful to teeth.

Crunching A Bunch

How many times do you crunch your lunch?
I have a hunch you crunch a bunch.
Ten crunches, 12 crunches; chew, chew, chew.
Carrots and apples and pretzels, too!

My Tooth Is Loose

A loose tooth can be very exciting—and a bit scary. Find out if any of your students have had a loose tooth. If none of your youngsters have lost baby teeth, invite an older child to discuss his tooth-losing experiences with your children. Encourage him to talk about when he first knew the tooth was loose, how long it took for the tooth to actually come out, what finally made it come out, and where he was when it broke loose. Students will enjoy the fact that you never know where you'll be when you lose a tooth. This is the essence of Grace Maccarone's *My Tooth Is About To Fall Out* (Scholastic Inc.). Read it aloud, if possible, or get your students to think of unfortunate places for a tooth to fall out. Enlarge the pattern on page 14 to create a tagboard cover for a big book to which each student can contribute a page. Duplicate only the outline of the enlarged pattern to create the book pages. Have each student contribute to the book by telling one unfortunate place for a tooth to slip out. Program his book page accordingly, and have him illustrate it and cut it out with your assistance. Staple the big book together and place it in your reading area.

Smiles All Around

This dental health game is a breeze to make and lots of fun to play. Photocopy page 14 for later use. Then use the pieces on page 13 to create a dental-health trail game similar to the one shown. Attach the animal designs to milk-jug lids so that they can be used as the game markers. Provide a film canister and three dried lima beans for imitation teeth—one of which has a small cavity drawn on one side. To play, have each of two players choose a game marker for his own and place it on Start. To take a turn, the first player tosses the beans from the film canister onto the gameboard. If all the imitation teeth are pearly white, that student moves forward three spaces: one for each tooth. But if the cavity is showing when the beans have been tossed, the player must go back to the nearest dentist for care. Players take turns tossing the beans and moving their markers. The first one to reach the big, bright smile wins that round.

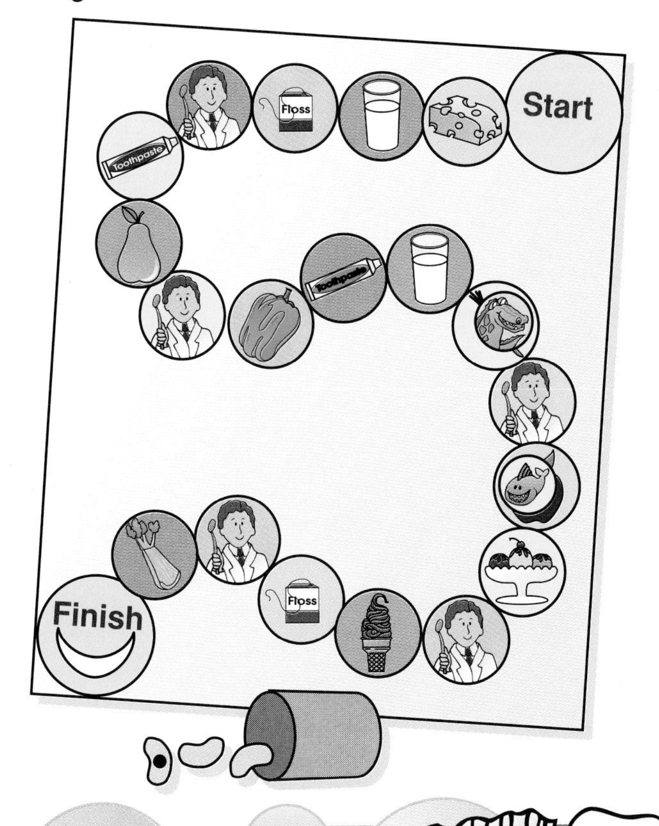

Kit And Caboodle

Make a few of these dental health kits so that your youngsters will be prompted to talk with their families about tooth care. To begin making a kit, spray paint all but the front and back of a large cereal box. So that it will completely cover the largest panels of the cereal box, enlarge a tooth design onto two sheets of poster board; then cut out both designs. Use markers or puffy paint to add a facial expression to each tooth cutout; then attach each one to the cereal box as shown. Staple the ends of a length of ribbon to the sides of the box to create a handle. When you have made a few of these boxes, fill them with things that will stimulate discussions about dental health. In each box you might include the following: a note to parents telling about the contents of the kit and their intended uses; side panels from a variety of toothpaste boxes secured on a ring; a copy of the song "Brushy, Brushy" (page 6); student-made minicollages on dental health themes; freebies from a local dentist; a tooth-related book (see the booklist on page 12); photos from a class field trip to a dentist's office; a copy of a floss-and-brush reminder; etc. When your dental health unit is winding down, give each student an opportunity to take a kit home for the evening and have some dental health fun with her family. When the kits are returned, replenish them and send them home with different students.

Toothbrush Bookmark Pattern

Use with "Tempting Tooth Tales" on page 9.

Dear Parent,

At school we have been studying dental health. Your child has learned that flossing, brushing, proper nutrition, and regular dental checkups are needed to keep teeth strong and healthy. Read a few of these books with your child to reinforce our dental health lessons. Use this toothbrush as a bookmark.

My Tooth Is About To Fall Out
By Grace Maccarone
Scholastic Inc.

Albert's Toothache
By Barbara Williams
E. P. Dutton

The Berenstain Bears Visit The Dentist
By Stan & Jan Berenstain
Random House, Inc.

Little Rabbit's Loose Tooth
By Lucy Bate
Scholastic Inc.

The Crocodile And The Dentist
By Taro Gomi
Scholastic Inc.

Bill And Pete Go Down The Nile
By Tomie dePaola
G. P. Putnam's Sons

My Dentist
By Harlow Rockwell
Greenwillow Books

Doctor De Soto
By William Steig
Scholastic Inc.

Loose Tooth
By Steven Kroll
Scholastic Inc.

Gameboard Pieces

Use with "Smiles All Around" on page 11.

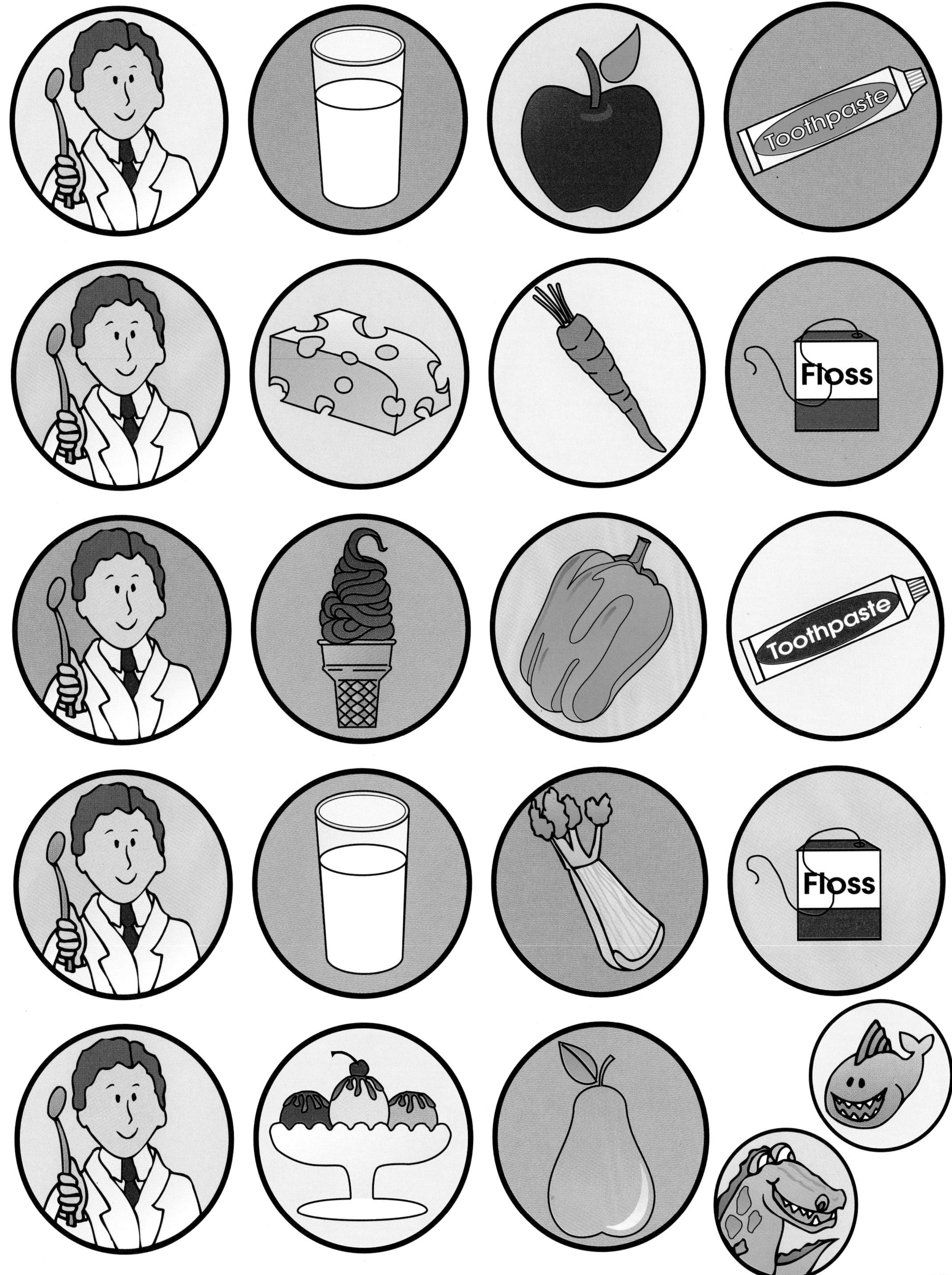

Book Pattern

Use with "My Tooth Is Loose" on page 10.

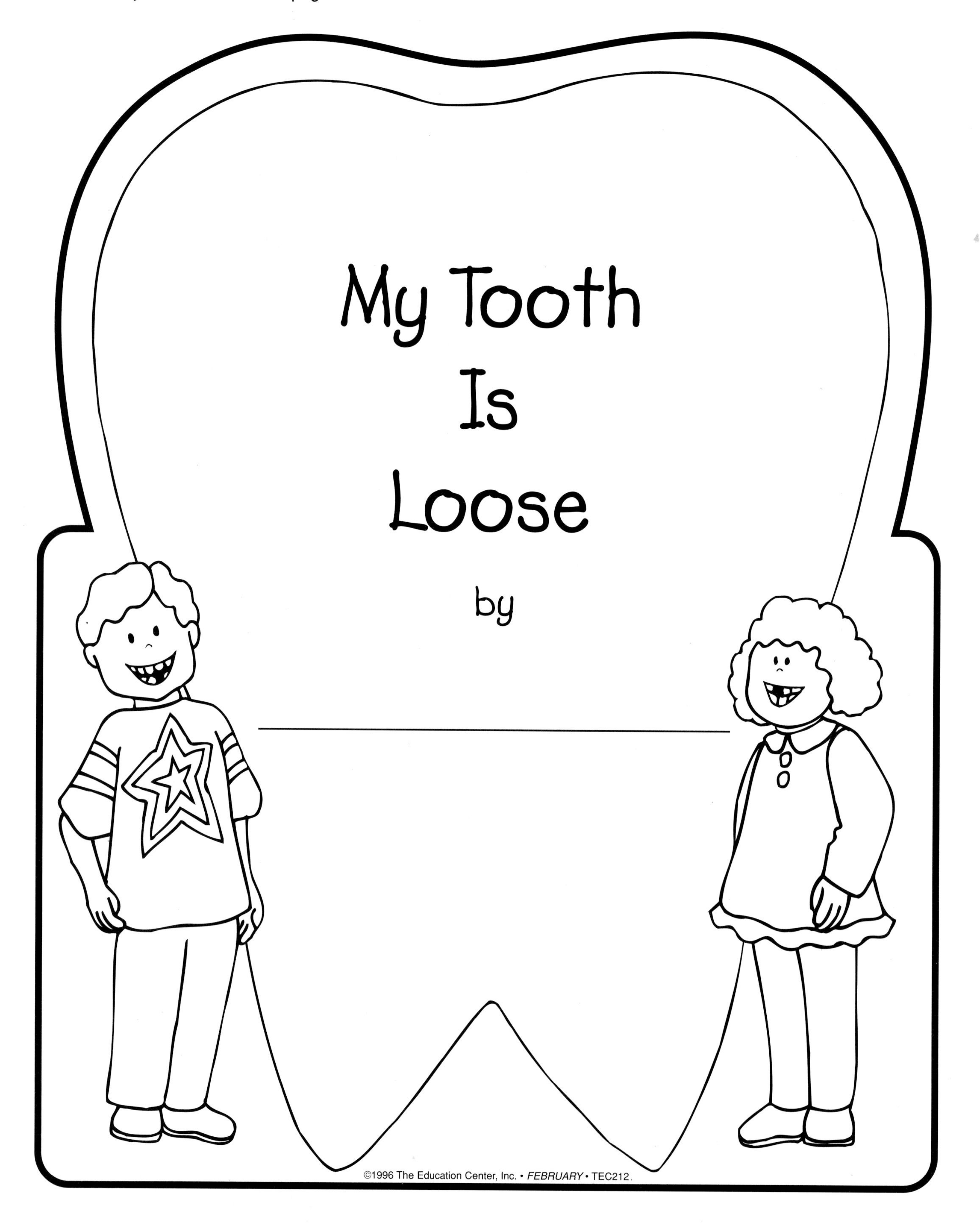

Headband Patterns

Use with "Our Friend The Dentist" on page 8. Use the dentist headband pattern with "Floss And Brush" on page 9.

Great Groundhogs

Youngsters will dig these fun groundhog-related activities and learning experiences.

ideas contributed by Barbara Backer

Looks, Lifestyles, And Legends

Share some of these interesting bits of information about the *groundhog*—also known as a *woodchuck* or *marmot*—to spark your students' curiosity about this curious, little creature.

What does a groundhog look like?

- Its body is covered with coarse, brown fur.
- It has very sharp teeth and claws.
- It grows up to 2 feet long and weighs from 8 to 12 pounds—about the size of a 10-pound bag of potatoes.

What are some habits of the groundhog?

- It is a *vegetarian*—it eats only plants, such as clover, grass, alfalfa, and vegetables.
- It digs an underground burrow or den.
- In the fall, it eats lots of food to fatten its body in preparation for *hibernation*—a long period of sleep during the winter.
- While it searches for food and eats, the groundhog often looks and listens for any signs of danger by rising up to sit on its haunches.
- At any sign of danger, the groundhog utters a shrill whistle to warn other groundhogs; then it scoots back into its own burrow.

What is the legend of the groundhog as a weather predictor?

- The legend of the groundhog and its shadow comes from the old European belief that a sunny day on February 2 is an indication of six more weeks of winter weather.
- It is believed that every February 2, the groundhog comes out of its burrow to look for its shadow.
- If it sees its shadow, the groundhog returns to its burrow to sleep for six more weeks. But if the groundhog does not see its shadow, spring will arrive early.

Counting Clover

Little ones will delight in helping this hungry groundhog puppet perform a clover countdown rhyme. To make a groundhog puppet, glue a pom-pom nose, wiggle eyes, and two brown felt ears to a brown sock. Cut five clover shapes from green felt. Place the clover cutouts on a flannelboard. Invite a child to put his hand into the sock puppet, then to move the puppet so that it appears to be opening and closing its mouth. While a small group of students recites this rhyme, have the groundhog "eat" one clover from the flannelboard. Repeat the rhyme four more times, substituting the underlined number word with *four, three, two,* and *one,* respectively. Then give another child a turn to be the groundhog. Continue in this manner until every child in the small group has had an opportunity to use the puppet. Then invite another group of students to play.

[Five] green clovers growing in the sun.
Groundhog took a bite. Yum, yum, yum!

Vegetarian By Nature

Classification skills will take root and grow as students sort out appropriate meal items for a vegetarian groundhog. To prepare, use an overhead projector to enlarge the groundhog on page 20 onto a sheet of poster board. Color the groundhog; then cut out a large opening for the groundhog's mouth. Attach the poster to the side of a large box to serve as a stand for the groundhog and a holder for its food. Put a supply of plastic models of insects and small animals—such as flies, spiders, mice, chickens, and snakes—into a large basket. Also put some plastic or silk grasses and small plants and some plastic vegetables into the basket. Place a box labeled "Animals" beside the groundhog poster. Before beginning play, remind students that groundhogs are vegetarians—they eat only plants and plant products such as grass, leaves, and vegetables.

Then divide your class into pairs of students. Ask one child in a pair to stand behind the groundhog poster to role-play the groundhog—she will receive items that are put in the groundhog's mouth. Then invite her partner to remove an item from the basket. If the item is one that a groundhog would eat—a plant or part of a plant—have the child place it in the groundhog's mouth. If the item is not one that a groundhog would eat, have the child place it in the box labeled "Animals." If a child places an inappropriate item in the groundhog's mouth, have her partner return the item so that she can place it where it belongs. Have the partners switch positions and continue until all the items are sorted correctly. Then return all the items to the basket and invite another pair of students to play.

When Will Spring Arrive?

A groundhog eats lots and lots of plants to fatten itself up for its winter hibernation. After its long winter's sleep, the groundhog leaves its burrow to search for food again. According to legend, the groundhog emerges from his burrow on February 2 to look for his shadow. Read aloud *Will Spring Be Early? Or Will Spring Be Late?* by Crockett Johnson (Thomas Y. Crowell Company). Then invite your little ones to become temporary weather predictors—in grand groundhog style!

To begin, explain the legend of the groundhog as a weather predictor to students. Then invite a child to pretend he is a hibernating groundhog in his burrow—the space under a table draped with several sheets. Give another student a flashlight so he can role-play the part of the sun. On a signal, have the groundhog awaken and emerge from his burrow. Ask the sun to decide whether or not he will shine on the groundhog. If he chooses to shine, have him turn on the flashlight and point it toward the groundhog. Encourage the groundhog to look around for his shadow and, upon spotting it, hurry back into his burrow saying, "Six more weeks until spring!" If the sun does not shine, encourage the groundhog to dance about and sing, "Spring will be here soon!" Then invite two different students to assume the roles of the groundhog and the sun. Repeat this game until each student has had the opportunity to play a role.

Give A Little Whistle

Your little groundhogs will stay alert and on the lookout with this action game. Purchase a class supply of inexpensive party-favor whistles. Thread a length of yarn through the loop at the end of each whistle; then tie the yarn ends together to create a necklace. Label each whistle with a different child's name. Outdoors randomly arrange several large plastic rings on the ground in a large, spacious area (plan to use one ring for every four to five students). Then randomly place some stuffed wild animals around the outer edges of the area. Give each child his whistle necklace to wear.

To play the game, invite one child to be the Danger Ranger—the person who holds up one of the animals and makes a threatening animal sound to represent danger. Have another child role-play the Great Groundhog—the person who detects the danger and warns the other groundhogs. Have all the other students stand in the rings pretending to be groundhogs in their burrows. Explain that—on the signal to "Come out"—all the groundhogs should leave their burrows and run around as if searching for food. Have the Danger Ranger wander about at random, then pick up an animal and make its sound. At that point, the Great Groundhog must blow his whistle to warn the other groundhogs of danger. Then all the groundhogs, including the Great Groundhog, should hurry back to their burrows. Continue the game, giving each child the opportunity to role-play the part of the Danger Ranger or the Great Groundhog.

I'm A Little Groundhog

Youngsters will enjoy reciting this catchy little rhyme while sporting their own groundhog masks. To make a mask, have a child color the underside of a paper plate brown; then have her cut a slit from the edge to the center of the plate. Help her overlap the cut edges so that the plate is formed into a shallow cone. Then staple the edges in place. Encourage the child to glue a pom-pom nose, a black construction-paper mouth, two brown construction-paper ears, and yarn whiskers onto the mask; then help her cut out two eyeholes from the mask. Tape a wide craft stick to the bottom of the groundhog mask. Invite each child to hold her mask in front of her face while she recites this rhyme.

I'm a little groundhog, so furry, furry, furry.
Looking round for my food. Oh, hurry, hurry, hurry.
When danger comes near me, I scurry, scurry, scurry
Right back to my burrow. Yes sir-ry, sir-ry, sir-ry!

Monday	Tuesday	Wednesday	Thursday	Friday
24 no	25 yes	26 yes	27	28
31	1	2	3	4

Watching The Weather

Weather-watching and shadow-viewing go hand in hand on Groundhog Day, so invite youngsters to do a little of both during the week leading up to and including this special day. In advance prepare a two-week grid on a sheet of poster board. Program the grid with the dates for the week prior to and the week including February 2—Groundhog Day. Label Groundhog Day with a small groundhog cutout. On each day, have the class go outdoors to check the weather. While outside, encourage students to look for their shadows. After returning to the classroom, ask students to describe the weather for that day. On the space for that day, draw (or have a student volunteer draw) a simple symbol or illustration to depict the weather. Then ask the children if they saw their shadows outdoors. Write the agreed-upon response—"yes" or "no"—in the calendar square for that day.

Before going outdoors on February 2, share with students a brief weather prediction based on a weather report for that day. Ask the children to predict, according to the weather report, whether they will or will not see their shadows when they go outdoors. Then, after the class makes its weather check and returns to the classroom, record the results on the calendar. After the two-week calendar is completed, compare the different types of weather the class observed over that time period and the number of days they saw their shadows versus the number they did not.

Groundhogs Are Great!

Youngsters will be able to express just how great they think groundhogs are when they help create this classroom display. For each child duplicate a copy of the groundhog on page 20 on white construction paper. Review some of the groundhog facts and myths (see "Looks, Lifestyles, And Legends" on page 16) with students. Then invite each child to use light brown tempera paint to sponge-paint his groundhog. After the paint dries, have the child cut out the groundhog. Ask the child to tell why he thinks the groundhog is a great animal. Write the child's dictated statement on a sentence strip. Display the groundhog cutouts and sentence strips on a grass green bulletin-board background. Title the display "Groundhogs Are Great!"

Groundhog

Use with "Vegetarian By Nature" on page 17 and "Groundhogs Are Great!" on page 19.

Shadows And Such

Focus the attention of your students on a delightful darkness—their shadows! With these activities that bring their darker images into the spotlight, youngsters will—beyond a shadow of a doubt—have lots of fun learning experiences!

ideas contributed by Barbara Backer

Shadow Showdown

Invite youngsters to cast their own shadows, then to cast a vote in this shadow-casting competition. To set up for the showdown, hang a solid white sheet on a wall to serve as a screen. A distance from the sheet, position a high-intensity flashlight or lamp, filmstrip projector, or other strong light source so that it shines onto the screen. Then gather a variety of items, some of which are opaque—such as a block or a stuffed animal; some translucent—such as a sheet of waxed paper or a plastic container; and some transparent—such as a clear plastic cup or a pair of eyeglasses. Near the sheet, place three boxes, each having a different color of construction paper—black, gray, or white—attached to it.

Before beginning the shadow showdown, introduce students to their shadows. Turn off or dim the classroom lights. Invite each student in turn to stand in front of the light source and observe his shadow. Ask him to describe his shadow—its color, shape, and movements. What happens when he moves closer to the light? Farther away?

Then begin the competition! Explain to students that when light does not pass through an item, that object will cast a dark shadow, like each of their shadows. Light may pass through other items, causing the shadows of these objects to be gray or barely existent. Have a student volunteer hold one of the items close to the screen in front of the light. As a class, decide whether the shadow cast by the object is black (or dark), gray, or mostly white with just an outline visible on the screen. Then ask the child holding the object to place it in the box with the appropriate color sheet attached to it. Continue with other volunteers until all of the items have been sorted. Afterward have a child place a blue ribbon on the box containing the objects that cast the darkest shadows—the shadow showdown champs!

A Day In The Sun

Now that youngsters have a basic understanding of how the position of a light source affects the shadow of an object, have them help perform this experiment simulating the different positions of the sun throughout a day. To prepare, spread out a white sheet on the floor. Set a two-liter plastic soda bottle on the center of the sheet. Tell students that during the course of a day, the sun changes positions in the sky. As the sun's position changes, the shadows of objects also change. To demonstrate, turn out or dim the lights; then invite a student to shine a flashlight at the bottle from near floor level. Ask the other children to comment on the resulting shadow. Then have the child with the flashlight slowly raise the light as high as possible, all the while shining it at the bottle. What happens to the bottle's shadow? At this point, ask the child to move the light directly over the top of the bottle. Now how does the shadow appear? Have the child continue to move the light over the bottle then slowly back down to floor level on the opposite side. Encourage students to discuss the changes they observe as the light moves from one side to the opposite side of the bottle. Then compare the movement of the flashlight to the sun's position in the sky during the morning, at noon, and in the evening. Now there's a shadow that's had its day in the sun!

Shadow Search

On a sunny day, take youngsters outdoors for a special walking tour to hunt for shadows. While on the shadow search, encourage students to look all around for as many shadows as possible. When a child spots a shadow, ask him to identify the object that casts the shadow. Encourage him to look for the light source (the sun) and to tell where it is. Guide him to realize that a shadow is always located on the side of the object opposite the light source.

After the shadow search, have little ones observe their own shadows while outdoors. Ask them to stand facing away from the direction of the sun. Can they see their shadows? Then have them face the direction of the sun. Now can they see their shadows? Again explain that a shadow is cast when the sun or light source is behind the object of the shadow. Also explain that as the sun's position in the sky changes, so do the sizes and shapes of the shadows cast by different objects and people. Remind students of the experiment with the light and shadow in "A Day In The Sun." Then, as a follow-up activity, read aloud and discuss *Bear Shadow* by Frank Asch (Simon & Schuster Books For Young Readers).

Shadow Train

Choo-Choo! Time to board the shadow train! While outdoors on a sunny day, invite children to play a game of Shadow Train. To prepare for the game, cut five different-colored sets of construction-paper squares, with each set containing four to five squares of the same color. Punch a hole in the top of each square; then thread a length of yarn through each hole and tie the ends of the yarn together to create a necklace.

To play the game, divide the class into groups of four to five students. Provide each student in a group with a necklace of the same color. Assign one child in each group to be the train engine; the other children will be train cars. Have the engines stand at a starting point. Ask the train cars to stand at a random distance from the starting point. On a signal, have each engine run to stand on the shadow of one of his group members. Then have the two group members hold hands so that a train is formed. Ask the engine to lead the train to tag another group member's shadow, then connect with him to lengthen the train. Have the children continue in this fashion until all the group members have joined the train. Then invite all the trains to move around the area in a variety of ways, observing their shadows and "choo-chooing" until they are signaled to stop. Then have a different student from each group assume the engine role and repeat the game. Continue play so that each child has the opportunity to be the shadow train's engine.

My Shadow

What happens to a shadow when the light source is removed? Youngsters will find out when they perform this action rhyme. Set up a screen and light source as described in "Shadow Showdown" on page 21. Divide your class into groups of two to three students. Then dim the lights and invite one group at a time to pantomime shadow actions to this rhyme while they stand in front of the screen. On the last line of the rhyme, turn off the light source; then ask students to comment on what happens to their shadows when the light goes out.

Sometimes my shadow's very small.
Sometimes it's very wide.
Sometimes my shadow's very tall.
Sometimes it likes to hide.

Sometimes it holds its arms up high.
Sometimes it holds them low.
Sometimes it moves like it can fly.
Sometimes it moves so slow.

My shadow follows me about.
But one thing I don't know.
When the shining light goes out,
Where does my shadow go?

Shadow-Seekers

The ever-popular game of hide-and-seek will take on a different shade of fun when youngsters play this version. To prepare, trace the outline of each of several familiar items—such as a pair of scissors, a block, a truck, a puzzle piece, and a rhythm instrument—on a different sheet of black construction paper. Make a few more outlines than the number equal to half the students in your class; then cut out the outlines to represent the shadows of the objects. Place the actual items in a large box or basket.

To play the game, divide your class into two equal groups of students. Have one group of students stand to one side of the classroom with their eyes closed, while each student in the other group hides a shadow cutout somewhere in the room. Also hide the extra shadows. Ask each shadow-hider to leave a small portion of each hidden shadow visible so that it can easily be found. After all the shadows have been hidden, have the other group of students open their eyes. Ask each child in that group to search until he has found one shadow. Have him take his shadow to the box to find the item to which it corresponds. After every child has found a shadow and its corresponding object, have each student in turn show the item and its shadow to the class. Then have the groups switch roles and repeat the game. Shadows, beware! Here come the shadow-seekers!

Shadow Match

Involve little ones in some more shadow play with this matching game. Make one copy of page 25 for each set of eight cards desired. Glue each set of cards to a sheet of tagboard. Cut the cards apart; then laminate them for durability. Turn the cards facedown on a table. A player will turn over two cards to look for a match—a figure and its corresponding shadow. If a match is found, that player keeps the cards. If the two cards do not match, the player returns them facedown to the table. Continue play with each subsequent player until all the matches have been found.

For younger children, you might leave all the cards faceup and have them match the figure to its shadow. For a variation, prepare sets of only the shadow cards, and have students take turns looking for shadow matches.

Use with "Shadow Match" on page 24.

Pancakes, Flapjacks, Griddle Cakes, And More!

Youngsters will be sizzling with excitement when you stir up a batch of pancake-related activities stacked with cross-curricular skills.

ideas contributed by Diane Gilliam and Mackie Rhodes

Griddle Cakes, For Goodness Sakes!

Tantalize your youngsters' senses when they help mix, then cook, the batter for these golden, delicious, aromatic pancakes—also called griddle cakes. In advance, gather a one-quart lidded plastic container, an electric griddle, a spatula, and the ingredients for the Palatable Pancakes recipe. Before beginning this activity, challenge youngsters to use their senses—sight, smell, taste, touch, and hearing—as they participate in the preparation and cooking of the pancakes. Preheat the lightly oiled griddle to 375°F. (As always, provide close supervision when using an electric appliance in the classroom.) Invite a different student to pour one of each of the ingredients into the container (excluding the toppings); then place the lid on the container. Pass the batter-filled container from student to student, having each child shake it in order to mix the ingredients. Then cook the griddle cakes on the heated griddle.

As the griddle cakes are being cooked, tell students that griddle cakes are also called pancakes and flapjacks. Do they know of any other names for griddle cakes? While the griddle cakes cool, have students participate in the activity described in "Ready, Set, Let's Eat."

Palatable Pancakes

(makes 10–12 small pancakes)

1 cup biscuit mix
3/4 cup milk
1 egg, beaten
1/2 tsp. oil
toppings (butter, syrup, fruit, powdered sugar)

Ready, Set, Let's Eat

Now that the pancakes are cooked and cooling, invite each student to get set to eat—by preparing a place setting for herself. For each student, provide a construction-paper placemat, a small Styrofoam® plate, a paper cup, a napkin, and a plastic knife, fork, and spoon. Have the students follow your lead as you give directions on arranging a place setting in the provided sequence.

1. Place the plate in the middle of the placemat.
2. Fold the napkin in half; then place it to the left of the plate.
3. Place the fork on the napkin.
4. Place the knife to the right of the plate.
5. Place the spoon to the right of the knife.
6. Place the cup near the top right corner of the placemat.

After each child has completed her place setting, serve her a short stack of cooled pancakes. Have her spread her choice of toppings on her pancakes; then invite each student to enjoy her treat with a cup of milk. The pancakes are ready! The table is set! Let's eat!

Making Sense Of It All

After youngsters take their last lip-smacking bites of flapjacks, help them summarize their sensory experiences with this description chart. On a sheet of chart paper, label each of five columns with the name for a different sense and a simple picture to represent that label. For instance, draw a mouth for the column labeled "Taste" and a nose for the "Smell" column. Ask students to recall what they experienced through each of their five senses as they prepared the pancake batter, then cooked and ate the pancakes. As students use descriptive words about their sensory experiences, write each word under the appropriately labeled column—such as "brown" and "round" under the column labeled "See," and "warm" and "sticky" under the "Touch" column. Display the completed chart with an animated pancake cutout titled "Pancakes Make Sense!"

What Is It?

The imaginations of your students will take on all sorts of shapes with this idea. In advance, prepare a number of pancakes, each with a different shape or form. For instance, a pancake might resemble a duck, an airplane, or a triangle. To make the different shapes, simply pour the pancake batter slowly onto a hot griddle in the desired forms. (Or, if preferred, cut a number of different forms from light brown construction paper to resemble odd-shaped pancakes.) Place each cooked pancake on a separate paper plate. During circle time, show students each pancake, asking them to name something that its shape resembles.

After having them study and comment on the odd shapes of pancakes, invite youngsters to create their own pancake shapes. Give each child a sheet of light brown construction paper and a pair of scissors. Ask her to draw a pancake in the shape of an object, animal, or any other item of her choice; then have her cut out the drawing along its outline. Have the child glue her pancake cutout onto a black, construction-paper frying pan cutout. Then use a white crayon to label the drawing according to the child's dictation. Display the pancakes with the title "What Is It?" Your little ones' creativity and insight may well delight you in this activity!

It's Pancake Time

Invite little ones to pantomime the actions to this song as they review the steps in preparing and eating pancakes.

(sung to the tune of "The Farmer In The Dell")

The batter we will stir.
The batter we will stir.
Heigh-Ho! It's pancake time!
The batter we will stir.

The batter we will pour.
The batter we will pour.
Heigh-Ho! It's pancake time!
The batter we will pour.

The pancake we will flip.
The pancake we will flip.
Heigh-Ho! It's pancake time!
The pancake we will flip.

The butter we will spread.
The butter we will spread.
Heigh-Ho! It's pancake time!
The butter we will spread.

The syrup we will squeeze.
The syrup we will squeeze.
Heigh-Ho! It's pancake time!
The syrup we will squeeze.

The pancakes we will eat.
The pancakes we will eat.
Heigh-Ho! It's pancake time!
The pancakes we will eat.

Lift The Flap For Flapjacks

Delight youngsters with a discussion of the sequence of events in the wordless book *Pancakes For Breakfast* by Tomie dePaola (Harcourt Brace Jovanovich, Publishers); then invite them to create these lift-the-flap books that sequence the steps in preparing flapjacks from mixing to eating. For each child, duplicate the sequence pictures on page 33. Then provide each child with a 12" x 18" sheet of construction paper that has been folded lengthwise and programmed with five evenly spaced lines on one folded side, as shown. Have the child cut along each line to the fold. Then help him label each resulting flap with a different numeral from one to six. Encourage the student to color each of the sequence pictures; then have him cut the pictures apart and glue each in sequence under the appropriate flap. Print the title "Flapjacks For Breakfast" on the back of the book. Then invite each student to share his book with a partner. Want to learn the steps in making flapjacks? It's as simple as lifting the flaps!

Flapjacks For Breakfast

FLOUR MILK

2 3 4 5 6

Pancake Painting

Before putting away your kitchen supplies and pancake fixings, mix up another batch of pancake batter for youngsters to use in a most unusual, but creative, way—as finger paint! In a large bowl, mix some pancake batter following the recipe for Palatable Pancakes on page 26, or follow the directions on a box of pancake mix. If desired, stir in a few drops of food coloring. Then pour a small amount of batter onto a large plastic plate for each child. Invite the child to spread the batter over the plate using his fingers; then encourage him to draw figures, shapes, letters, or numbers in the batter. To add a bit of variety to his finger paint, have the student add a few squirts from squeeze bottles of syrup and margarine to his batter. Then have him swirl and mix the substances together. Extend this activity by providing a few kitchen utensils—such as spatulas, forks, and spoons—for youngsters to use for their batter writing. What an icky-sticky, oh-so-fun way to paint!

The Pancake Place

Your dramatic-play center will be hopping with activity when you convert it into the most popular pretend restaurant at school—The Pancake Place! Post a sign labeled "The Pancake Place" near your dramatic-play area. Arrange the furniture in the center to resemble a restaurant setting. Spread a tablecloth over a table; then place an artificial flower arrangement in the center of the table. Have available an apron, a notepad and pencil, several copies of a menu, and a wallet or purse. Stock the center with items such as plastic utensils and dishes, pots and pans, recycled syrup and margarine containers, play money, a cash register, and a supply of homemade play dough (see recipe). Then invite small groups of children to participate in the operation and patronage of The Pancake Place using the provided supplies and props. The boundless opportunities for dramatic play will keep this pancake place hopping at all hours of the day!

Homemade Play Dough

1 cup flour	2 tsp. cream of tartar
1 cup water	1 Tbsp. cooking oil
1/2 cup salt	food coloring

Mix all the ingredients in a saucepan over low heat, stirring constantly until a dough forms. Cool the dough on waxed paper. Store the cooled play dough in an airtight container.

The Pancake Man

Do you know the Pancake Man? He's the one with the frying pan! When little ones participate in this combination song and game, they will practice skills in cooperation, listening, and problem solving. Have youngsters form a circle. Ask a volunteer to be It and to stand in the middle of the circle with his eyes closed. Have the other students sing this song while passing a small frying pan behind their backs and around the circle. After singing the last line, have the last child to receive the passed pan hold it behind his back. Then invite It to open his eyes and guess which child he thinks is the Pancake Man—the child holding the pan. If desired, provide descriptive clues to help It guess correctly. When the Pancake Man is identified, have him exchange places with It. Continue the game in this manner so that each child has the opportunity to be It or the Pancake Man.

(sung to the tune of "The Muffin Man")

Oh, do you know the Pancake Man?
The Pancake Man?
The Pancake Man?
Oh, do you know the Pancake Man?
He has the frying pan!

From Pan To Plate

Transferring pancakes from pan to plate will provide students with some action-packed fun when they play this progressively challenging game. To prepare, cut five pairs of pancake rounds from light brown felt. Hot-glue each pair together along the edges, leaving a small opening to insert a few spoonfuls of uncooked rice. After adding the rice, hot-glue the edges of the opening together. If desired, hot-glue a yellow, felt pat of butter onto each pancake. Then place the felt pancakes in a large plastic frying pan. Place a plastic plate a distance from the pan. Invite each child, in turn, to pick up each pancake from the pan and toss it onto the plate. On the child's next turn, challenge him to scoop each pancake from the pan with a spatula, and then carry it (or toss it) to the plate. On another turn, ask each child to put one pancake in the pan, then pick up the pan and try to toss the pancake from the pan to the plate. Can youngsters think of other challenging ways to transfer the pancakes from the pan to the plate? However it's done, it's a lot of fun!

Flip The Flapjack

Students will flip over this flapjack memory game. Duplicate ten copies of the flapjack-pair patterns on page 34 on brown construction paper; then cut out the patterns. Glue a yellow, construction-paper pat of butter to the center of each cutout. Then program the other side of each cutout in a pair with matching letters, color dots, shapes, designs, or numerals. If desired, laminate the cutouts for durability. Randomly place the cutouts, butter side up, on a sheet of black bulletin-board paper to represent a griddle. Give each student in a small group a small paper plate. Then invite a player to flip over two flapjacks. If a match is found, have the child put the matching flapjacks on his plate. Otherwise, have him return the flapjacks to the griddle; then invite the next child to take his turn. Continue play until all the matches have been found. Then set the griddle game up for the next group of youngsters to play.

Pancakes That Measure Up

How do your pancakes measure up? Ask students this question when they use these paper pancakes as nonstandard units of measure in this activity. In advance, duplicate five copies of the pancake patterns on page 34 (for a total of ten pancakes) on light brown construction paper for every two students in your class. Cut out the patterns; then top each with a glued-on yellow construction-paper pat of butter. Place each set of ten paper pancakes in a zippered plastic bag. Then, for every two students, duplicate a copy of the necklace patterns on page 34 on construction paper. Cut the necklace patterns apart. Divide your class into pairs of students; then give each child in a pair either the counter or the recorder pattern to color and personalize. Punch a hole in the top of each decorated necklace pattern and thread a length of yarn through the hole, tying the ends together to create a necklace. Have each student wear his necklace so that each pair has an identified counter and recorder.

Provide each pair of students with a copy of the recording sheet on page 35. Equip each counter with a bag of paper pancakes and each recorder with a pencil and a copy of the recording sheet. Explain that the counter will place and count the number of paper pancakes needed to measure each object listed on the recording sheet. The recorder will then write that number in the appropriate space on the sheet. After each pair of students has completed its recording sheet, have all the pairs compare their results with the findings of the others in the class. Discuss why some of the results may differ—such as measuring the long versus the short end of a table, or selecting a different size block to measure. In this activity, these pancakes sure measure up!

The Shape Of Things

Invite your pancake lovers to sharpen their visual-discrimination skills in a shape hunt, then to illustrate their findings in a class book. To prepare the book covers, glue a strip of black construction paper onto each side of a wooden paint-stirring stick. Then cut three nine-inch circles from black construction paper. Glue the end of the stick between two of the black circles; then glue the edges of the two circles together so that a shape resembling a frying pan results. Set the remaining black circle aside for later use. For the book pages, cut an eight-inch circle from a sheet of manila paper for each child. Explain to youngsters that most pancakes assume a round shape when the pancake batter is poured into the pan for cooking. Then ask each child to look around the classroom to find an item that is round in shape—like a pancake. During group time, invite each youngster to show or name the round item that he found.

Then have each child illustrate his round book page with a picture of something that is round. Write his dictated statement about the round object on his page. Stack the completed pages on top of the frying pan–shaped cover with the handle of the pan extending to the left. Top the book with the remaining black circle—the front cover. Use a hole puncher to punch a hole through the pages and covers on each side of the pan handle; then bind the book using metal rings. Write the title "Round Like A Pancake" on the front cover using a white crayon. Place the book in the reading center for students to enjoy.

Slapjacks, Clapjacks, Flapjacks!

Create a rollicking rhythm with a knee-slap/hand-clap pattern as students recite this bouncy chant. Have students slap their knees twice, then clap their hands together once, repeating the actions over and over to create a steady rhythm. Then have students say this chant to the rhythm of their slapping and clapping. After saying the chant the first time, have the children repeat it twice, replacing the underlined word first with *flapjacks,* then with *griddle cakes.*

[Pancakes] are sticky.
[Pancakes] are sweet.
[Pancakes] are yummy.
Good to eat!

Yummy in the morning.
Yummy at night.
Open your mouth and
Take a bite!

Sequence Pictures

Use with “Lift The Flap For Flapjacks” on page 28.

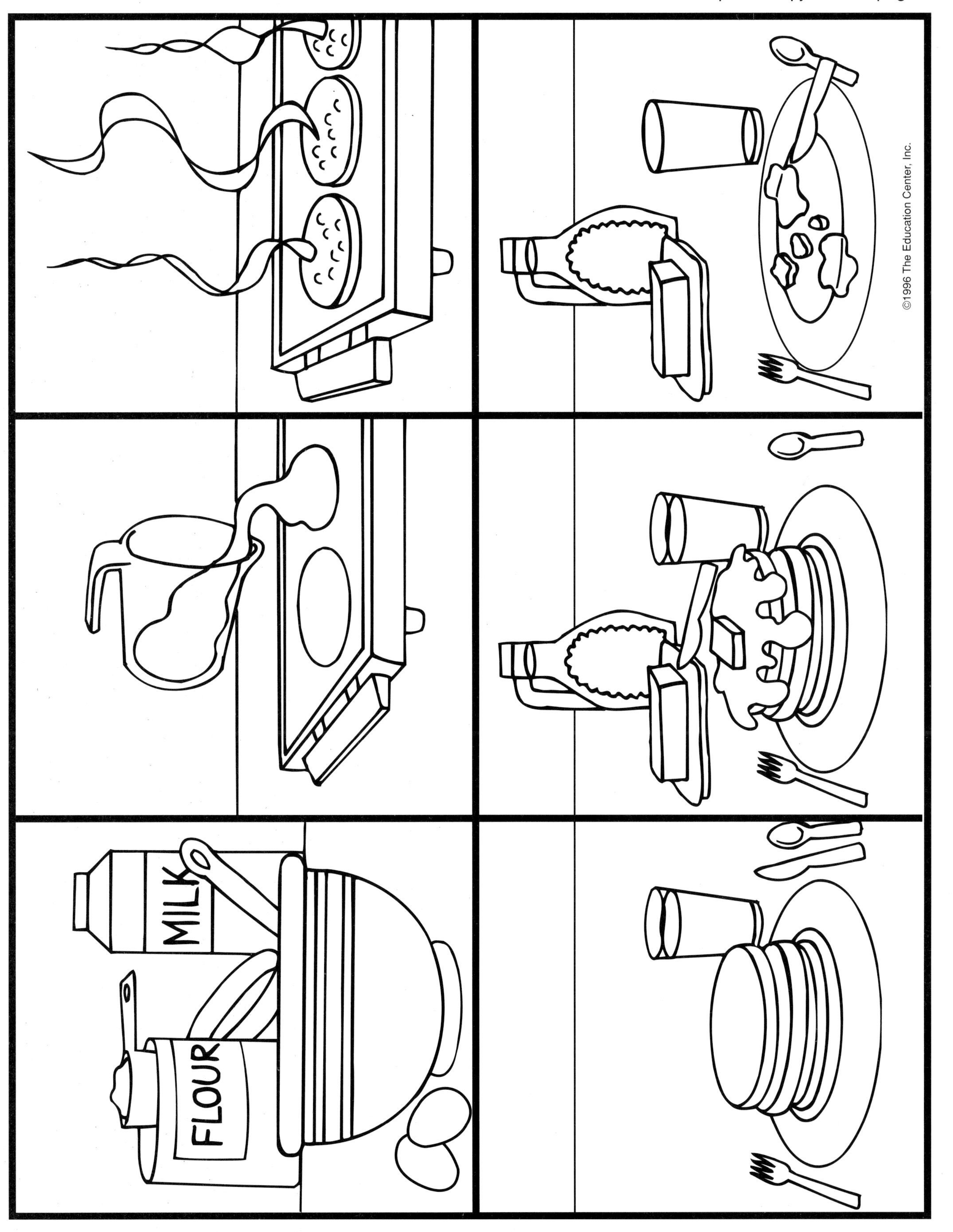

Necklace And Pancake Patterns

Use the necklace and pancake patterns with "Pancakes That Measure Up" on page 31. Use the pancake patterns with "Flip The Flapjack" on page 31.

Recording Sheet

Use with “Pancakes That Measure Up” on page 31.

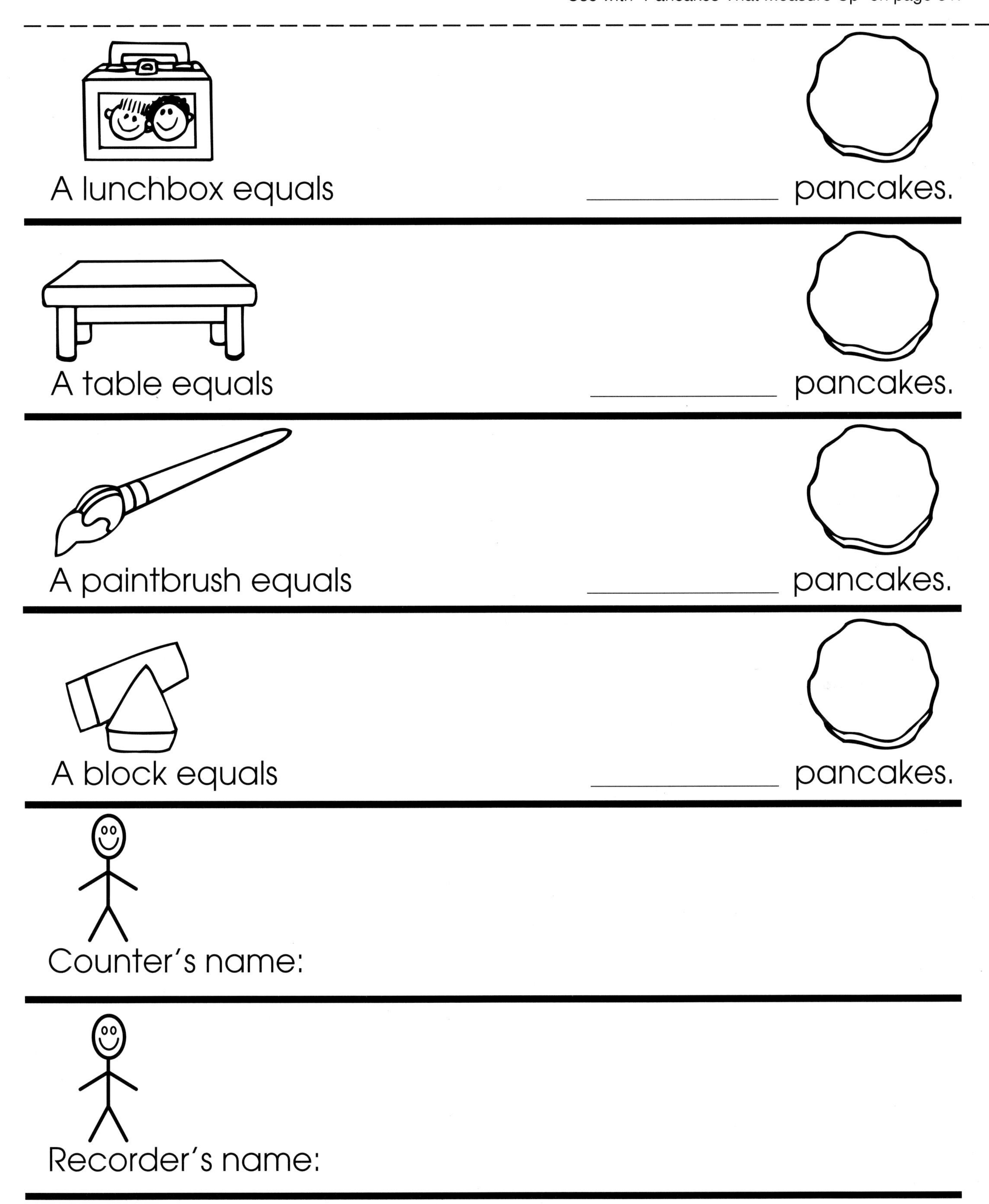

A lunchbox equals ____________ pancakes.

A table equals ____________ pancakes.

A paintbrush equals ____________ pancakes.

A block equals ____________ pancakes.

Counter’s name:

Recorder’s name:

"VALEN-TASTIC"!

Excite your little ones during this time of affection with lots of activities dealing with the magic of Valentine's Day. You'll love using the following collection of ideas to practice skills from across the curriculum.

by Angie Kutzer

HAPPY HUNTING

Have a happy heart hunt. While the children are away, hide at least three heart cutouts for each child. When the children return, ask them to each find three hearts. Encourage youngsters to gather on the carpet as soon as they have found the hearts. To practice one-to-one correspondence, have each child return his heart cutouts to you one by one as he names a loved one for each heart. To conclude this activity, pass each child a heart as you mention one of his lovable characteristics. Love makes the world go 'round!

COOPERATIVE CARDS

Spread a little love around your school with this assembly-line activity. To prepare, make several heart-shaped tagboard patterns and gather pencils, construction paper, scissors, stickers, and an assortment of art supplies such as glue, lace, and markers. With your students, make a list of people around your school to whom they would like to send valentines—office workers, custodians, administrators, and book buddies. After reading the story *Valentine Cats* by Jean Marzollo (Scholastic Inc.), divide your class into five groups: tracers, cutters, writers, artists, and postal workers. Have the tracers trace the heart patterns onto construction paper. Continuing on down the assembly line, have the cutters cut out the tracings and the writers copy "We Love You!" onto the heart cutouts. Encourage the artists to decorate the cutouts before passing them along to the postal workers to be folded and stamped (with stickers or rubber stamps). When all the cards are finished, accompany your students throughout the school to distribute them. Now *that's* special delivery!

CUPID NEEDS A HEART

Add a little twist to the traditional game of Pin The Tail On The Donkey by pinning a heart on Cupid! Enlarge the pattern on page 42 and tape it to your board. Give each child a heart cutout labeled with his name on the front and with two-sided tape attached to the back. Blindfold one child at a time, spin him around several times, and turn him to face the board. Instruct the child to walk toward Cupid and without feeling around, attach his cutout where he thinks Cupid's heart should be. When everyone has had a turn, bring in some math lingo by comparing whose heart is the closest to and the farthest from the target. Are there any hearts that are the same distance apart? Will Cupid have a heart—in the right place?

MISSING HEARTS

To practice alphabet recognition and sequence, label each of 26 heart cutouts with a letter of the alphabet. Display these hearts in order in your pocket chart. Sing the alphabet song while pointing to each letter in turn. Have the children shut their eyes while you remove a letter. See who can identify the missing heart. As their letter-recognition skills improve, try removing more than one letter at a time. This activity can also be adapted to work with shapes, colors, and numbers. With lots of practice, your children won't miss a beat!

MATCHMAKERS

This whole-group activity works on visual discrimination and matching skills while your children eagerly wait to be your secret valentines. To prepare, you'll need pairs of heart cutouts about the size of an 8 1/2" x 11" sheet for each child in your class. Make each pair identical either by drawing a pattern on them or coloring them the same way. (A great time-saver would be to cut these hearts out of wallpaper sample books!) Distribute the hearts to the children, keeping one heart of each pair for yourself. Have the children join in the rhyme below as you hold up one of the hearts. Continue until everyone has made a match or until interest wanes.

My friend gave me a valentine,
But signed it as "Guess Who?"
Our hearts are just alike, you see.
So stand up if it's you!

HEART ART

Your little ones will be hopping all the way home to give this special valentine to someone they love. Share the story *Guess How Much I Love You* by Sam McBratney (Candlewick Press) and follow up with the construction of these huggable hares. Fine-motor skills will be exercised along with lots of direction-following!

To prepare for this activity, use the patterns on page 44 to create the following cutouts for each youngster: one large brown paper heart (for the ears), one large brown felt heart (for the face), two medium brown paper hearts (paws), one small black paper heart (nose), and two small green paper hearts (eyes). Place the materials needed for one rabbit in a separate file folder for each child. Also place in each file folder a 12" x 18" sheet of red construction paper, two 22mm wiggle eyes, and a sentence strip. Distribute glue, scissors, and chalk to tables.

After sharing the story, give each child a file folder and explain that everyone will be making a valentine by listening, watching, and copying what they see you do. Explain and model each of the following steps for your group. Assist as necessary.

Directions:

1. Fold the large brown paper heart in half vertically and cut on the folded line.
2. Put the red paper on your table so that it is TALL, not wide.
3. Glue the brown half-hearts (ears) to the top of your paper so that curves are facing the outer edges of the paper.
4. Glue the brown felt heart (face) upside down onto the bottom of the ears.
5. Glue the green hearts where the eyes should be.
6. Glue the wiggle eyes on top of the green hearts.
7. Glue the black heart (nose) near the middle of the face where the heart's curves meet.
8. Use chalk to draw whiskers out from the nose.
9. Accordion-fold the sentence strip using two-inch folds. (Talk them through this step by repeating, "Fold up, turn over, fold up, turn over, fold up," etc.)
10. Unfold and copy the message, "This much!"
11. Glue the middle two sections of the strip to the red paper below the rabbit's face.
12. Glue the two medium brown heart cutouts (paws) sideways to the ends of the strip so that the paws touch when the strip is accordion-folded.

To finish, program the bunny ears for each child as shown. Your children will love this honey-bunny!

WHERE'S CUPID?

Review letter, number, and shape recognition as your youngsters search for Cupid. Use the hearts from "Matchmakers" on page 37 and program an appropriate number of them with letters, numbers, shapes, or a combination of these. Attach the tops of the hearts to your board in two or three rows. Reduce the Cupid pattern on page 42 so that it is smaller than these hearts. Have your students hide their eyes while you hide Cupid behind a heart. Choose a child to name a heart. Lift the heart named. Is Cupid there? If so, reward the student with a sweet treat such as Hershey's Kisses®. If not, give another child a turn until Cupid is found. Once he's found, hide him again! Continue until each child has received a treat.

PASS IT ON

Hearts will beat wildly as your students wonder who will get the "Victory Valentine" in this circle-time game. Purchase inexpensive valentines (one per child) and attach a piece of candy to each. On one valentine, attach something extra—maybe a candy bar, pencil, or sticker. This will be your "Victory Valentine." Have your children sit in a circle. Give a valentine to one child and start the rhyme below. The child will pass the valentine around the circle until the rhyme stops. When the rhyme is finished, the child holding the valentine keeps it and leaves the circle. You then give another valentine to the next child and begin the rhyme again. Play continues until one child is left. Present him with the "Victory Valentine."

Little, little valentine
Passing from their hands to mine.
'Round the circle you will go.
Who will get you, we don't know.
Little, little valentine,
I hope that you will be mine!

HEARTSTRINGS

Math skills abound in this valentine activity. All you need is a skein of red yarn, scissors, a heart drawn on your chalkboard, and the book *A Village Full Of Valentines* by James Stevenson (Greenwillow Books). Share this delightful story about how different animals in a village prepare for and celebrate Valentine's Day. At the end of the story, Gus the tailor has used excess red string to make a heart around the entire village for one huge valentine to everyone.

After you read the story, direct your children's attention to the heart drawn on the board. Explain that they will pretend to be Gus and that this is the size heart they need to go around their village. Let each child come up and pull from the skein of yarn, estimating how much it will take to go around the heart. Cut the yarn when she thinks she has enough. As children wait for the next step, encourage them to use their yarn to make a heart on the floor. Each child comes up again and helps you measure her string against the heart. Ask the class for a conclusion using measurement terms—*longer, shorter, the same as, more,* or *less.*

Now actually measure the heart with a strand of yarn and cut the correct length. Use this for children to compare with their strands. Are theirs longer or shorter? Ask them to find out whose strand is the closest to the correct length. Your youngsters will enjoy measuring with their own heartstrings!

CHOOSE A MATE

There are several histories regarding the beginning of Valentine's Day. The earliest one recorded in English tells of birds choosing their mates on this day. Relay this information to your youngsters and get ready to fly! Use the following adaptation to the traditional circle and singing game of Bluebird. Students hold hands in a circle with arms up, making arches between the children. One child is selected as the first bird. He "flies" in and out of the arches while everyone sings the song. At the end of the verse, he taps another child and they both begin to fly while the song is sung again. Continue until there is a classroom full of lovebirds!

REDBIRD

(sung to the tune of "Bluebird")

Redbird, Redbird, through my window,
Redbird, Redbird, through my window,
Redbird, Redbird, through my window,
Oh, won't you be my friend?
(Oh, we are all good friends! *[last time through]*)

ROLL, COUNT, AND EAT!

Seasonal candies like conversation hearts, valentine-colored M&M's®, or cinnamon hearts can provide excellent counting practice for your little ones. Pair up your students. Give each pair a plate containing two spoonfuls of candy and a die. The children will take turns rolling the die, naming the number rolled, counting the same number of candies, and eating them! The partners see to it that numbers are named correctly and that candy is counted correctly.

MY TEACHER LOVES ME!

Wondering what to do for your little ones this Valentine's Day? Give them a keepsake that will last a lifetime–a special photo of the two of you. In advance have a parent volunteer, another teacher, or an assistant take a photo of you with each child. Once the pictures are developed, use a heart-shaped cookie cutter and a pen to trace around each one. Then cut out the shapes. On Valentine's Day, duplicate page 45 on white construction paper for each child. To make a valentine, have each child color, cut, and assemble the puzzle to reveal the mystery message. Help him glue the puzzle to another piece of construction paper and read the message. Later, while your students are out of the room, go by and mount each heart-shaped photo on the correct card; then sign and date it. The children are sure to put this photo card in their scrapbooks to enjoy for years to come!

VALENTINE DRAMATICS

Encourage oral communication skills by having groups of six students perform the following rhyming skit. You will need to gather a few props before you teach the rhyme. Give Child One a valentine with candy attached. (Child Two doesn't need anything.) Give Child Three a handful of valentines. Give Child Four five valentines and Child Five a valentine gift bag. The child playing the part of Teacher needs some sort of teacher prop (pointer, glasses, etc.). Align five chairs in a row facing your students. Have children one through five sit in the chairs in numerical order.

Introduce your children to the rhyme by reading it aloud and demonstrating the motions. Rehearse the rhyme a few times so that your students can begin to join in. Now you're ready! Have your entire class say the rhyme as the Teacher stands behind the chairs and taps each actor when it is his turn to perform the motions. When they're finished, the first group goes back to the audience so that more stars can shine!

FIVE LITTLE CHILDREN ON VALENTINE'S DAY

(to the rhythm of "Five Little Jack-O'-Lanterns")

Five little children sitting at their seats—	*(Children sit and look down.)*
The first one said, "My valentine has treats!"	*(First one shows his valentine to group.)*
The second one said, "I don't have a valentine."	*(Second one pokes out his lip and whines.)*
The third one said, "Here, have some of mine!"	*(Third one happily hands second child some cards.)*
The fourth one said, "Aren't valentines fun!"	*(Fourth one tosses valentines in air.)*
The fifth one said, "Hey, look! I have a ton!"	*(Fifth one looks inside bag with fourth child.)*
"[Kissing sound]" went the teacher and	*(Teacher blows kiss to audience.)*
"[Kissing sound]" went the crowd.	*(Audience blows kisses back to teacher.)*
Five little children stood up and took a bow.	*(Children take a bow.)*

VALENTINE SHAPES

Change piggies to valentines in this fun rhyme for the flannelboard. Cut out the valentines on page 43 and attach a piece of felt to the back of each. With your students, review the traditional nursery rhyme "This Little Piggy Went To Market." Show each valentine character to your children, ask them to name its shape, and have them find things around the room with the same shape. End the activity by reciting the rhyme at the right several times while children take turns manipulating the valentine pieces on a flannelboard. Leave the pieces on the board and encourage your children to perform the rhyme during center time.

This little valentine is a circle.
This little valentine is square.
This little valentine is a triangle.
This little valentine has hair!
This little valentine said,
"Happy Valentine's Day!"
To everyone, everywhere!

Cupid Pattern

Use with "Cupid Needs A Heart" on page 37 and "Where's Cupid?" on page 39.

Valentine Pieces

Use with "Valentine Shapes" on page 41.

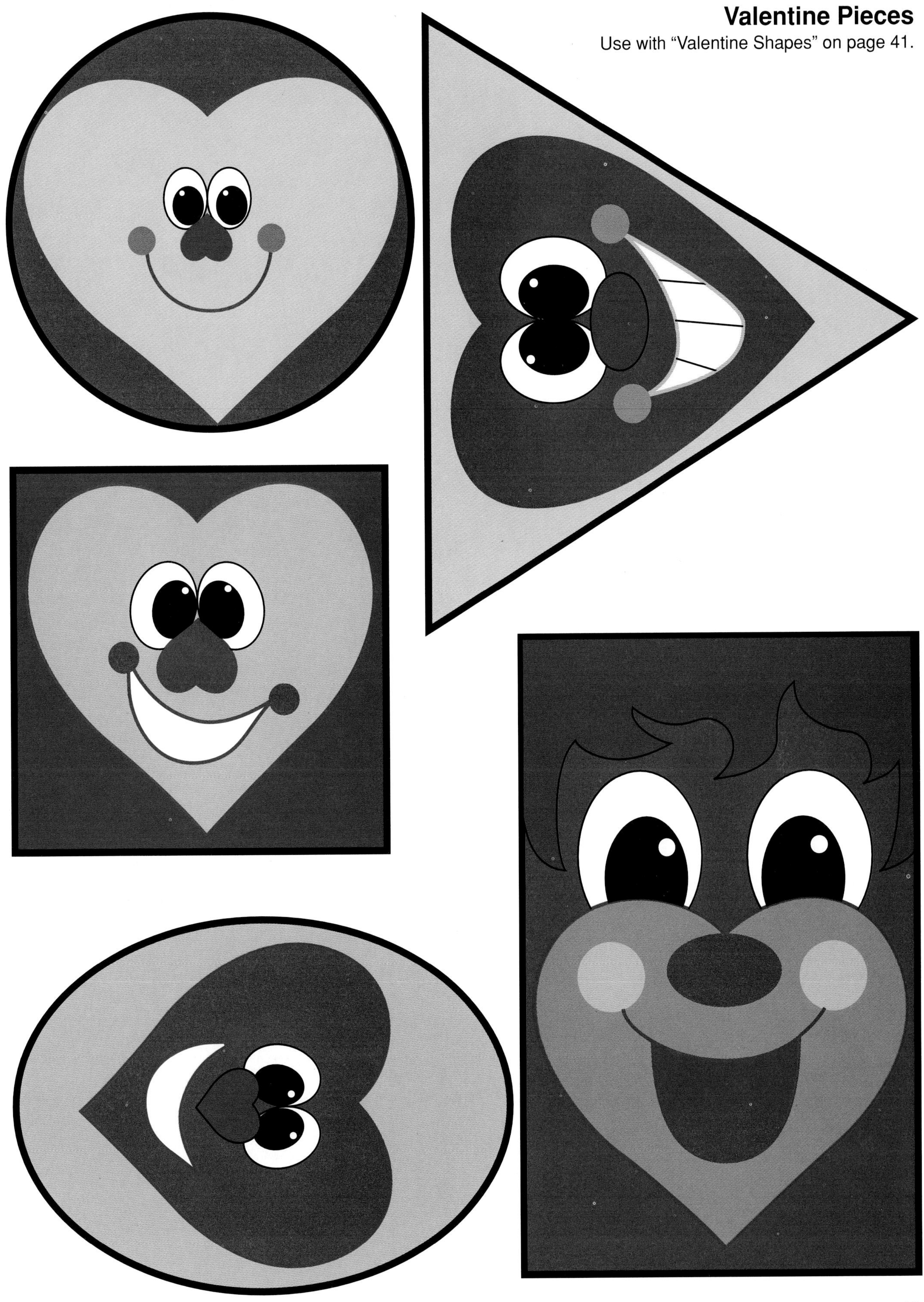

Heart Patterns

Use with "Heart Art" on page 38.

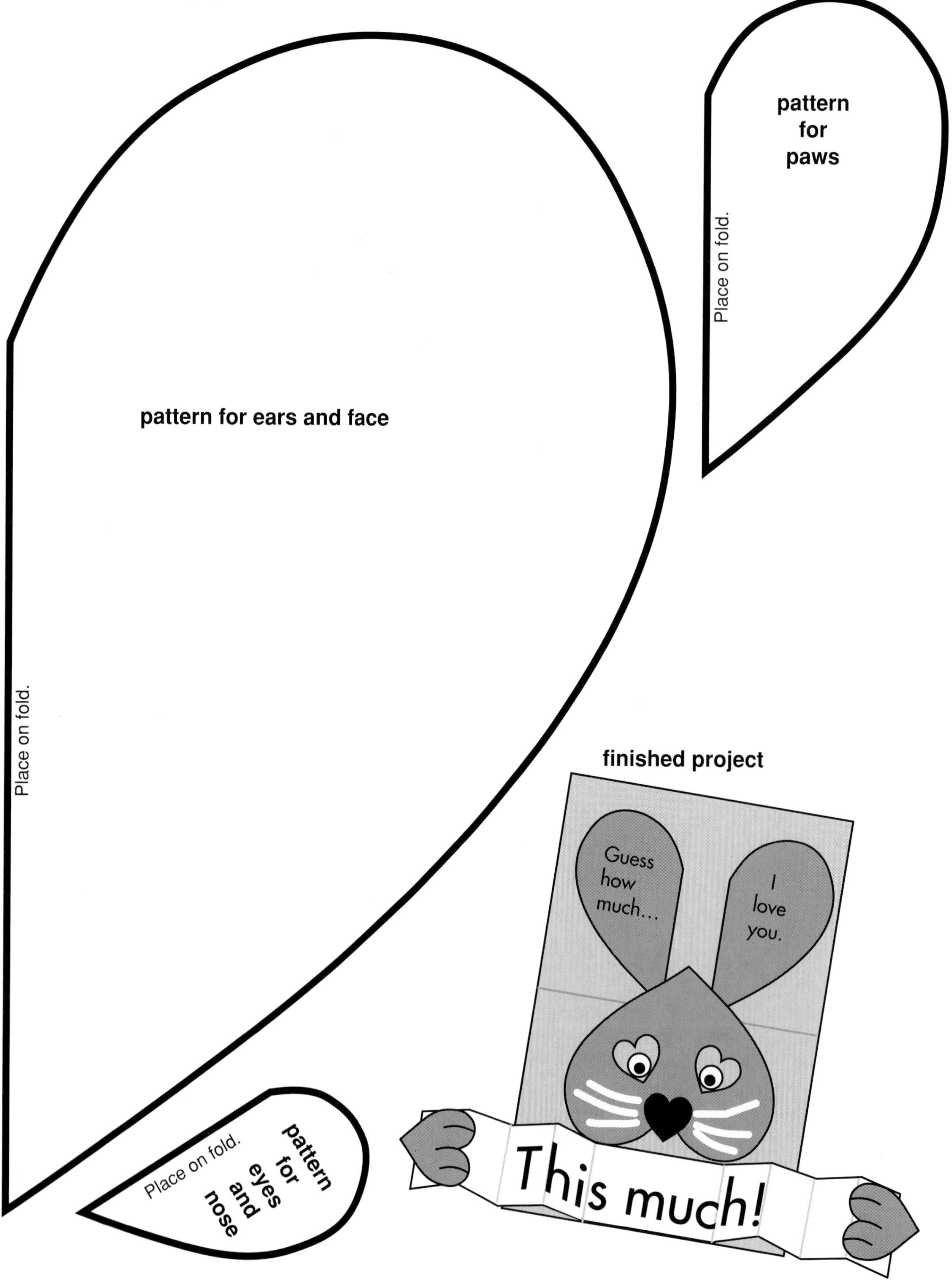

Use with "My Teacher Loves Me!" on page 40.

Give A Cheer For Cherries!

George Washington made the cherry a famous and favorite fruit for this time of year. Check out these cherry activities to get your little ones involved in music, math, language, cooking, and art.

ideas contributed by Jan Brennan and Ada Hanley Goren

Taste Some Cherries

Begin your unit by bringing in some cherries for students to examine and taste. Fresh cherries are not in season in most places during the winter, but jars of maraschino cherries are available year-round. Give each youngster a few cherries to taste. Then make a list of student-generated words to describe cherries, such as *red, round, sweet,* and *soft*. Ask how many youngsters have tasted cherries before. Have any of them eaten fresh cherries? Show a picture of a fresh cherry from the encyclopedia or a nonfiction book about fruit. Discuss the differences between fresh cherries and cherries bought in the jar. Finally ask youngsters to brainstorm a list of foods that are cherry-flavored.

A Cheery Cherry Booklet

After having youngsters list as many cherry-flavored foods as they can, invite them to complete the reproducible booklet on page 50. For each child, duplicate a copy of page 50 on white construction paper. Cut the pages apart on the bold lines. Prepare and provide the necessary art materials: red, construction-paper squares; glue; crayons; cinnamon candies; red watercolor paint; paintbrushes; cherry-flavored Lifesavers®; a red stamp pad; and gelatin paint (a mixture of two cups of cold water and three ounces of cherry-flavored gelatin powder). Read each page of the booklet to your students; then assist each child in illustrating her pages as follows:

Page 1: Glue a few red paper squares to the bowl. Color the pie. Glue a few cinnamon candies to the top of the pie.
Page 2: Paint red watercolor paint over the liquid in the glass.
Page 3: Finger-paint the ice pop with the gelatin paint. Color the candy roll. Glue a cherry Lifesavers® candy near the candy roll.
Page 4: Personalize the happy face to look like you. Press one finger onto the red stamp pad; then add fingerprint cherries to the page.

When each page is complete and dry, help each child assemble her pages in order. Bind each child's pages between two 4 1/2" x 6" red, construction-paper rectangles. Print the title "A Cherry Cheer" on each child's front cover. Encourage little ones to share their booklets with one another; then invite them to take their booklets home to "read" to their families.

Granola Greats With A Cherry On Top

(makes 18 servings)

1 cup rolled oats
1/3 cup wheat germ
1/4 cup coconut
1/4 cup sunflower seeds
1/4 cup powdered milk
1 teaspoon cinnamon
2 tablespoons honey
2 tablespoons vegetable oil
1 teaspoon vanilla
two 8-ounce containers cherry yogurt
Cherries

Mix together the first six ingredients. Add the honey, oil, and vanilla; then mix well. Place a foil liner in each cup in a muffin tin. Half-fill each cup with the granola mixture. Bake at 375°F for about 8 minutes; then cool. Spoon one tablespoon of yogurt on top of each granola cup. Finish off each snack with a cherry on top!

Please—With A Cherry On Top

After making "Granola Greats With A Cherry On Top," your youngsters will have experienced a treat with the ultimate topping—a cherry. Explain that the phrase, "Please—with a cherry on top?", is used as an extra-nice way to make a request. Give your students a chance to employ that phrase with this game, played similarly to Mother, May I?

Line up a small group of children on one side of your classroom or playground. Position yourself at some distance from the children. Give a movement command—such as "Take three giant steps," "Tiptoe ten times," or "Take five hops forward"—to each child in turn. Before performing the movement, the child must say, "Please—with a cherry on top?" If the child forgets to use that key phrase, he cannot move forward. As each child reaches you, reward his efforts—and good manners—with a cherry-scented sticker or a cherry-flavored candy.

A Bowl Of Cherries

Counting practice will be just a bowl of cherries with this fun activity. For each child in a small group, cut a set of red, construction-paper circles to represent cherries. (Depending on the age level and abilities of your students, make either 10 or 20 cherries per child.) Provide a paper or Styrofoam® bowl and a set of cherry cutouts for each child. Then teach youngsters one of these rhymes, depending on their counting abilities. Have each child place the appropriate number of paper cherries in his bowl as the rhyme is recited. After performing the rhyme as a group, give each youngster a chance to recite it solo.

Rhyme 1:

One cherry, two cherries, three cherries, four.
Five cherries, six cherries, seven cherries, more.
Eight cherries, nine cherries, ten cherries in.
Take them out and count again!

Rhyme 2:

One cherry, two cherries, three cherries, four.
Five cherries, six cherries, seven cherries, more.
Eight cherries, nine cherries, ten cherries—go!
Eleven, twelve, thirteen—whoa!
Fourteen, fifteen, sixteen—my!
Seventeen, eighteen, nineteen—why?
Twenty cherries is our goal!
Twenty cherries in the bowl!

George Washington And The Cherry Tree

The legend of young George Washington telling the truth after having chopped down his father's cherry tree is an inspirational story about honesty. Share the version of this story found in *The Children's Book Of Virtues* edited by William J. Bennett (Simon & Schuster, Inc.), or retell the story in your own words. Then invite pairs of students to role-play young George and his father. Encourage little ones to come up with their own dialogue as they act out the story. After every child has had a turn to play either George or his father, teach students this song to help them remember the story.

Cherry Blossom Art

Follow up the story of George Washington and the cherry tree by having little ones make cherry-tree pictures. To prepare artificial cherry blossoms, shake some popped popcorn in a paper bag with some cherry gelatin powder or dry pink tempera paint.

If possible, show youngsters a picture of a cherry tree in bloom from an encyclopedia or a nonfiction book. Then have each child draw or paint the trunk and bare branches of a tree on a sheet of blue construction paper. Give each child a small handful of pink popcorn—cherry blossoms—to glue onto his tree's branches. After the glue dries, display the finished projects on a classroom bulletin board with the title "Cherry Blossom Art" for a hint of spring to come!

Sally

Do You Know Who Chopped The Tree?

(sung to the tune of "Do You Know The Muffin Man?")

"Do you know who chopped the tree,
Chopped the tree, chopped the tree?
Do you know who chopped the tree?"
Dad asked of George one day.

"Yes, I know who chopped the tree,
Chopped the tree, chopped the tree.
Yes, I know who chopped the tree,"
Honest George did say.

"It was I who chopped the tree,
Chopped the tree, chopped the tree.
It was I who chopped the tree.
I'm sorry, but it's true."

"Thank you, George; you told the truth,
Told the truth, told the truth.
Thank you, George; you told the truth,"
Said Dad. "I'm proud of you!"

Cherries And Cherry Pits

Written by Vera B. Williams
Published by Greenwillow Books

Share the stories in this book that are told by Bidemmi, a little girl who loves to draw. Each story ends with its characters eating cherries and spitting out the pits. Read each story at a different time; then try these related activities.

Something Special

The first story in *Cherries And Cherry Pits* tells of a daddy who brings home a white bag with something special inside for each of his four children—cherries, of course! Follow up this story with something special for your students. In advance, cut 26 large circles from red construction paper. Label each circle with a different letter of the alphabet. Place all these cherries in a white paper lunch bag. If you do not have an alphabet strip displayed in your classroom, print the alphabet on sentence strips for this activity.

After sharing the story, bring out the white bag and tell students that you have something for them. Ask each child, in turn, to reach into the bag and pull out a paper cherry. Have him identify the letter printed on his cherry and match it to the same letter on the alphabet strip. Ask a more advanced student to locate an object in the classroom with the same beginning sound as the letter on his cherry.

Who's Got The Cherry?

The third story in *Cherries And Cherry Pits* is about a brother who brings home a surprise for his little sister—yes, a cherry! He holds out both closed fists and asks her to guess which hand the surprise is in. Follow up this story with a game of Cherry, Cherry, Who's Got The Cherry?

Use a small, red object—such as a button or a bead—to represent a cherry for the game. Have the children stand in a circle, facing the center. Ask each child to stand with her hands cupped together behind her back. Explain that you will walk around the perimeter of the circle, touching each child's hands, and that you will drop the cherry into one child's hands. Tell the children not to let anyone know whether or not they receive the cherry. After a complete pass around the circle, ask, "Cherry, cherry, who's got the cherry?", and see if anyone can guess which child is holding the cherry. After the recipient of the cherry is identified, he will be the next one to walk around the circle and drop the cherry into another child's hands.

Note To The Teacher: Use with “A Cheery Cherry Booklet” on page 46.

How Sweet It Is!

Use the irresistible temptation of chocolate to get your little cocoa connoisseurs involved in some sweet learning experiences.

ideas contributed by Ada Hanley Goren and Suzanne Moore

Let's Check Out Chocolate

Share the following facts about chocolate with your students. If possible, show the photographs in the book *Vanilla, Chocolate, And Strawberry: The Story Of Your Favorite Flavors* by Bonnie Busenberg (Lerner Publications Company) to help youngsters understand how chocolate is grown and processed.

- Chocolate is made from cacao beans, the seeds of the cacao tree. These trees grow in many areas near the equator, including Nigeria, the Philippines, Mexico, and Venezuela. Help youngsters locate these countries on a world map or a globe.
- Cacao beans grow inside a hard seed-pod, which looks sort of like a football-shaped coconut. The seedpod changes color from green to gold to purple as it ripens.
- To make chocolate, cacao beans are removed from the seedpod, then roasted and ground. This process makes the fat inside the beans—cocoa butter—melt, and the beans turn into liquid chocolate.
- Americans eat more than ten pounds of chocolate per person per year! Europeans eat twice that amount.
- Chocolate is added to some medicines to make them taste better.
- Some people are allergic to chocolate. Be sure to check for allergies among your students before proceeding with any activities in this unit that involve eating chocolate.

All Kinds Of Chocolate

The liquid chocolate that results from the roasting and grinding of the cacao beans is the basis for all kinds of chocolate. Without any additives, it becomes what we call baking chocolate. Varying amounts of sugar added to liquid chocolate make semisweet and sweet chocolate. Adding sugar and condensed milk makes milk chocolate.

Conduct a taste test of various kinds of chocolate. Duplicate the record sheet on page 55 for each child. Then provide each student in a small group with a bit of unsweetened baking chocolate, a semisweet chocolate chip, and a milk chocolate chip. Have each child taste one type of chocolate at a time, then draw a happy or sad face in the corresponding space to indicate whether or not he liked it. Encourage youngsters to count and compare how many children in their group liked and disliked each chocolate sample. Then repeat the taste test with the remaining groups of students.

A Chocolate Chant

Teach youngsters this rhyming and rhythmic chant about some chocolate-flavored favorites. Have youngsters chant the rhyme as they perform the accompanying movements or jump rope.

Chant	Movement
Chocolate, chocolate	
Tastes so sweet—	*(Rub tummy.)*
How much chocolate can I eat?	*(Palms up; shrug gesture)*
Chocolate pudding,	*(Hold up one finger.)*
Chocolate chips,	*(Two fingers)*
Chocolate ice cream—double dips,	*(Three fingers)*
Chocolate candy,	*(Four fingers)*
Chocolate bars,	*(Five fingers)*
Chocolate cookies in cookie jars,	*(Six fingers)*
Chocolate syrup,	*(Seven fingers)*
Chocolate drops,	*(Eight fingers)*
Chocolate in my lollipops,	*(Nine fingers)*
Chocolate cream pie,	*(Ten fingers)*
Chocolate shake,	*(Wiggle all ten fingers.)*
Too much chocolate	
means a tummy ache!	*(Bend over and hold tummy.)*

Our Chocolate Choices

Document each of your student's preferred chocolate foods in a big book that may become the class favorite—bar none! First review the chocolate foods mentioned in "A Chocolate Chant." Then ask students to list all the other chocolate foods they can think of. Print their responses on a sheet of chart paper; then ask each child to choose his favorite chocolate food from the list. Have him illustrate his choice on a 12" x 18" sheet of white construction paper. Print the name of the food below his drawing to complete his class-book page.

Then create this clever cover for the book. Cut two 12" x 18" pieces of poster board. Wrap one piece of the poster board—gift-wrap style—with aluminum foil. Then wrap a 12" x 18" sheet of construction paper over the center of the foil-covered poster board and tape that in place, so that the cover resembles a giant, wrapped candy bar. Write the title "Chocolate Choices" on the cover. Stack the pages between the front cover and back cover (the other piece of poster board). Bind the book on the left side. Mmm...mouthwatering reading!

Chocolate Choices

by Mrs. Moore's Class

Dippin' Into The Chocolate

Enough talk about chocolate—it's time to eat some! Help youngsters prepare this yummy chocolate snack.

Crunchy Apple Dippers
(serves 24)

2 12-ounce packages of milk chocolate chips
6 apples, cored and quartered
2 cups chopped nuts

In a heavy saucepan, melt the chocolate chips over medium heat, stirring constantly until smooth. Remove from heat and cool until warm. Pour the chocolate into a pie pan. Pour the chopped nuts into another pie pan. Push a craft stick into each apple quarter. Dip the apple quarter into chocolate, and then roll it in the nuts.

Cold Or Hot?

Chocolate's not only good to eat, it's good to drink, too! But do your students prefer it cold or hot? Have them sample some chocolate drinks both ways; then create this three-dimensional graph to display the results. Before sampling the drinks, collect a classroom supply of clean, empty, individually sized chocolate-milk cartons and the same number of six-ounce Styrofoam® cups. Cut the bottom from each milk carton. Then photocopy each child's school picture.

Provide small samples of cold chocolate milk and warm hot cocoa for each child to taste. Have him choose an empty milk carton if he prefers the chocolate milk or a Styrofoam® cup if he prefers the hot cocoa. Have him glue his photocopied picture to the side of his chosen container. Then staple the cartons and cups in two separate rows on a bulletin board to create a graph. Add the title "Do You Like Chocolate Cold Or Hot?" Encourage youngsters to count the containers in each row to determine which drink was the class favorite.

A Hot-Fudge Fiesta

There's one chocolate treat that's cold *and* hot—a hot-fudge sundae! Invite youngsters to create these artificial sundaes; then send them home with an invitation for parents to attend an ice-cream social at school—complete with hot fudge and a selection of chocolatey toppings. (Be sure to serve other topping flavors, too.)

To prepare, purchase a class supply of nine-ounce clear plastic cups, plastic spoons, two-inch Styrofoam® balls, and 1/2-inch Styrofoam® balls. Dip each of the smaller Styrofoam® balls in red acrylic paint (to represent cherries) and allow them to dry on a sheet of waxed paper overnight. Cut some brown cardboard into tiny bits (to represent nuts); then prepare the recipe for Hot-Fudge Paint.

To assemble his sundae, have each child place a two-inch foam ball into a cup, then drizzle on two or three spoonfuls of Hot-Fudge Paint. Have him add a foam-ball cherry and a sprinkling of cardboard nuts before the paint dries. Write each child's name on the handle of his spoon; then wedge it into his cup. Let each child's finished project dry overnight before sending it home with a copy of the invitation on page 55.

Hot-Fudge Paint
Mix together 1 1/4 cups flour, 1 1/3 cups water, 5 tablespoons salt, and 5 tablespoons dry brown tempera paint.

Don't Smudge The Pages!

Little ones may be tempted to chomp some chocolate while enjoying these two books about the favored flavor! Share each book—along with the accompanying activity—for a literature connection to the chocolate confection!

The M&M's® Counting Book

Written by Barbara Barbieri McGrath
Published by Charlesbridge Publishing

This photo-illustrated book uses those colorful chocolate candies we all know and love—M&M's®—to illustrate some simple math concepts. Read the book to one small group of youngsters at a time. Then bring out a large bag of M&M's® and invite students to either follow the book's text or follow your lead in demonstrating counting and other math skills suitable to their level. (Note: New packages of M&M's® no longer contain tan candies mentioned in the book. Substitute blue M&M's® for tan.) After some counting, sorting, and shape creation, invite youngsters to munch on those mathematical M&M's®!

Sam's Surprise

Written by David Pelham
Published by Dutton Children's Books

This unique, lift-the-flap book is guaranteed to have your youngsters grossed out and giggling! In the story, Samantha has prepared a box of birthday chocolates for her brother and his pals. The rhyming text hints at the yucky surprise filling in each candy.

Before sharing the story, prepare a game of Candy Concentration. Duplicate the candy patterns on page 55 as many times as desired on brown construction paper; then cut out all the patterns. Program the back of each cutout to make matching pairs for practice with the skill of your choice—upper- and lowercase letters, numerals and number words, or rhyming words. Laminate the cutouts and store them in an empty candy box.

After reading *Sam's Surprise,* tell youngsters that you have a surprise for them as well. Pull out a box of real chocolates and pass it around, inviting each child to choose a chocolate to sample. While students are eating, show them the Candy Concentration game and explain how to play. Have a small group of children place all the candy cutouts (programmed side down) on a tabletop. Each player, in turn, turns over two candies, attempting to locate a matching pair. If his two candies match, he may keep them. If they do not match, he turns them back over and another youngster takes a turn. Play continues until all the matches have been found.

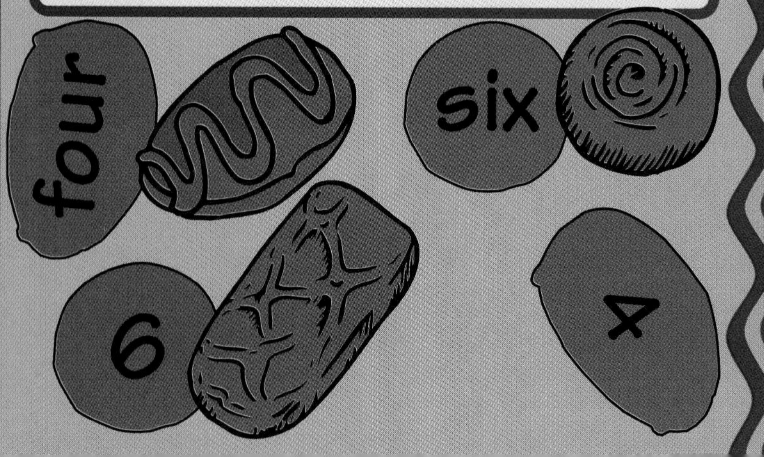

Record Sheet

Use with "All Kinds Of Chocolate" on page 51.

Name ____

baking chocolate	semisweet chocolate	milk chocolate

Invitation

Use with "A Hot-Fudge Fiesta" on page 53.

Chocolate—gooey, fudgy, hot!
This is chocolate. (No, it's not!)
But come to school and you will see
Real fudge sundaes for you and me!

Please join us for
an ice-cream social on

______________________________.
(date)

Chocolate-Candy Patterns

Use with *Sam's Surprise* on page 54.

SPECIAL DELIVERY

A little transformation here and another one there. Before you know it, your classroom will take on many of the attributes of a busy post office, and your youngsters will zip merrily from one curriculum-related activity to another.

ideas contributed by Carrie Lacher

The Scoop On Mail Delivery

Find out what youngsters already know about post offices, mail, and mail carriers. Ask students if letters, cards, or packages ever come to their homes. Then ask a series of questions about where the mail is left, who puts it there, what a postal carrier's job is like, and what's inside a post office. Jot children's responses on chart paper.

Reading and discussing Gail Gibbons's *The Post Office Book: Mail And How It Moves* (HarperCollins Children's Books) is a great way to give students' comments even more focus. If you have access to an overhead projector, display each book page on a screen as you talk with the children about the amazing journey of a piece of mail. Afterward have students dictate the new things they have learned about the postal service, as you add these new bits of information to the chart.

Up Close And Personal

There's no better place to start your postal unit than in the hub of postal activity—your local post office. To prepare nametags, reduce the envelope pattern (page 62) to approximately 3" x 5" and program it with your name and your school's address in the upper left corner; then reproduce one envelope for each child. Label each envelope with a child's name and your school's address. Then have each child choose and attach a sticky stamp (see "Sticky Stamps" on page 58) to his envelope nametag. Laminate each child's tag, punch a hole in each upper corner, and thread it with yarn. Now that's a first-class nametag!

Before your visit, have each child dictate his name and address while you write it on a postcard; jot a note on each child's card. Take the cards along on your trip. Arrange to have each child bring along enough money to purchase a postcard stamp. During your tour, snap lots of photos—especially when youngsters purchase stamps and drop their postcards in the mail slot. After the trip, have students help you draft a letter of thanks to the postal workers who made your field trip possible. Enclose a photo with the letter of thanks when you mail it. Display the remaining photos for inspiration throughout the rest of your post office study.

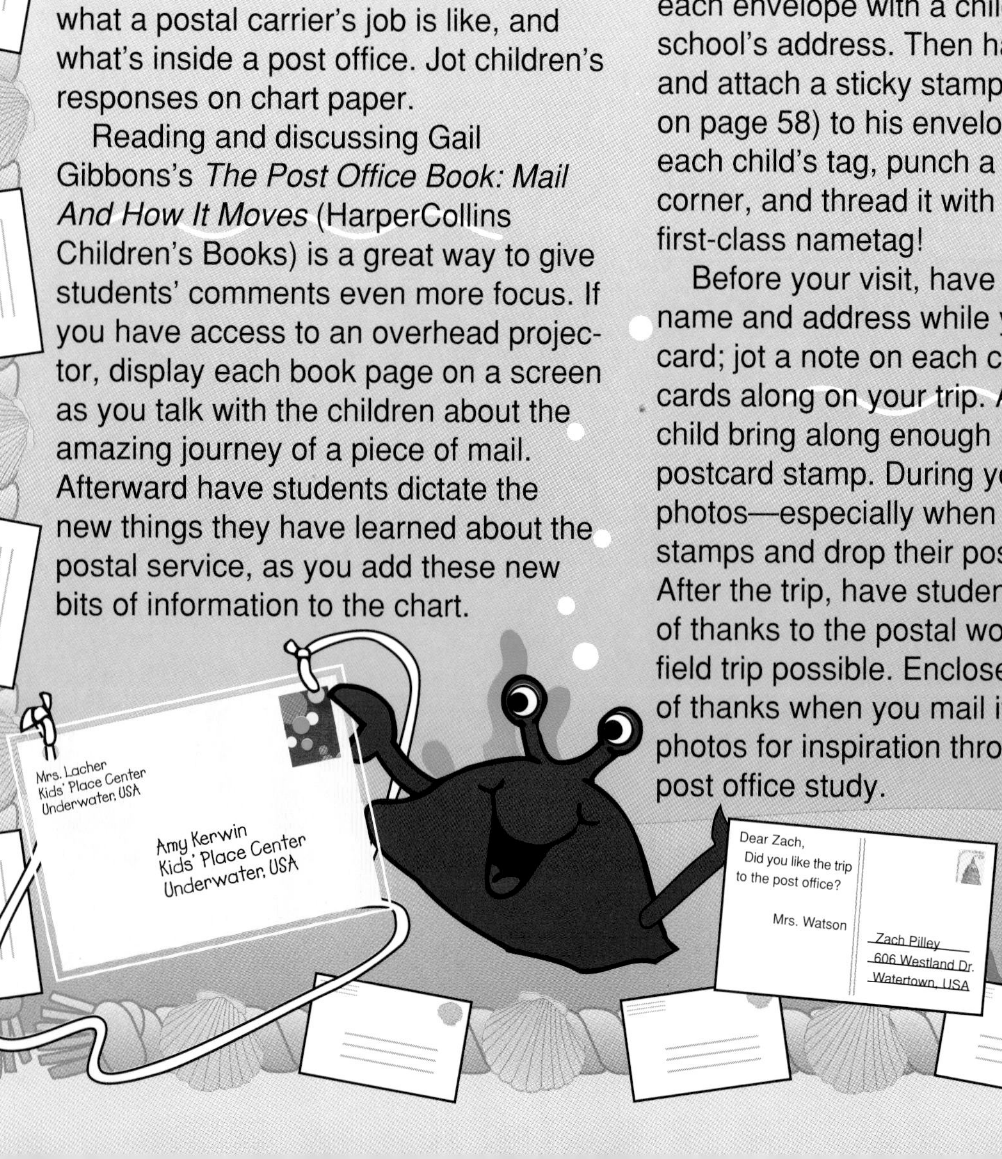

Uniforms For All

It won't take students long to notice—either during their visit to the post office or later as they examine the photos taken there—that postal workers' uniforms include the U.S. Mail logo. Since there will be lots of opportunities for students to role-play postal workers' jobs, make sure your students are dressed for the part. On white construction paper, duplicate the postal workers' badges (page 64), one badge for each student. Ask each child to color his badge and glue it to a 1 1/2" x 8" construction-paper strip. Fit the badge to the child's arm, trimming the excess strip and taping it to form a band that will stay on the student's upper arm. Whenever students are role-playing postal workers, suggest that they dress the part by wearing their badges.

First-Class Postal Worker

A Classy Post Office

Now that your students not only have become postal experts but they also look the part, invite them to use their knowledge to create their very own classroom post office. Gather your little ones together for a brainstorming session (near where the pictures of the field trip are displayed). List their suggestions for what should go into their post office. Guide the discussion so that students conclude they could use items such as junk mail, used stamps, rubber stamps, ink pads, envelopes, paper, a scale, play money, a cash register, address labels, return address labels, markers, pens, tape, and empty boxes for mailing. During the next few days, encourage students to help you set up a post office area that contains many of these things, as well as student-made stamps (described in "Sticky Stamps" on page 58), enlargements of the classroom post office logo (page 65), and copies of the envelope pattern on page 62. Periodically refer students to the photos of your post office field trip, to refresh their memories about which supplies should be grouped together in their post office. Invite school dignitaries to a ribbon-cutting ceremony when your post office is complete. So that each youngster will look the part, remind students to wear the postal worker badges described on this page for the occasion.

First-Class Post Office

STAMPS

Mailboxes

Now that you've got a post office right in your classroom, create a couple of other props to complete the effect. First make a postal collection box. Seal a large cardboard box shut, and place it in your art area, requesting that students help paint it blue. When the paint is dry, stand the box on end. Cut both a flap for the mail chute and an access door for classroom postal workers to use. Attach a pickup schedule (programmed with times suggested by the students) between the two flaps; then attach a colored enlargement of the postal logo on page 65 to the opposite side of the collection box.

Then help students make individual mailboxes. For each child, trim the top off a clean, dry, quart-size milk carton. Assist each child in covering his mailbox with construction paper. Duplicate the flag patterns (page 64) onto red construction paper so that each child has one. Have each child cut out his flag and attach it to his carton with a brad so that it can be raised and lowered. Encourage the child to decorate his mailbox as he desires and label it with his name. On your copier, enlarge and duplicate each child's school photo. Trim it to about a 2 1/2-inch square and attach it to the mailbox as a privacy flap. Arrange the entire group of student mailboxes in one convenient location.

Pickup
3 P.M.

Postmarked And Perfect

Adults may not give them a second thought, but the variety and visual interest of stamps will not be lost on your students. Ask each student to trim used stamps off mail from home, after asking her parents' permission. When you have gathered a sizable collection, spread the stamps out on a tabletop where several students can examine and discuss them at once. (Provide a few magnifying glasses, so students can take a really close look.) Ask your students to think of categories that the stamps could be sorted into. Then provide plenty of time for students to sort the stamps.

Sticky Stamps

Classroom postal workers will be happy to keep their mail moving when they use tasty homemade stamps. Gather an interesting assortment of gift-wrap papers trimmed to 8" x 10" sheets. Then make some nontoxic stamp adhesive. Place a small package of flavored gelatin powder into a bowl, pour in one cup of boiling water, and stir until the gelatin dissolves. When the mixture has cooled sufficiently, invite children to brush it lightly onto the unprinted sides of the gift wrap. When the paper has completely dried, invite children to cut stamp-size rectangles from it or cut it into strips to make books of stamps with construction-paper covers. As your students work in their classroom postal center, they'll never have to scrounge around for a stamp. They'll have oodles of them to lick and stick.

Moving The Mail To A Beat

The mail in your classroom will soon be moving to a musical beat when you introduce these lyrics to your children. Encourage students to wear their postal badges (see "Uniforms For All" on page 57) as you sing and dance.

I'm A Little Letter

(sung to the tune of "I'm A Little Teapot")

I'm a little letter,	*(Indicate your height with your hand.)*
Nice and fat.	*(Spread arms out to your sides.)*
Here is my address.	*(Pretend to write across your torso.)*
Here is my stamp.	*(Make a square with your fingers and place it over your heart.)*
Drop me in a mailbox;	*(Mime dropping mail into a slot.)*
Then watch me go—	*(Zip flat hand across your body.)*
Sending my love	*(Hug yourself.)*
Around the globe.	*(Draw a large circle in the air with both arms.)*

Postal Carrier's Tune

Borrow a mail carrier's bag, jacket, and hat from your local post office during your postal unit. You'll also need at least one piece of unopened junk mail per child. Pass each child a piece of junk mail while the child you have selected to be the first postal carrier is dressing for the part. Have students sit in a circle holding their mail and singing the first verse as the postal carrier walks from child to child collecting the mail. Sing the first verse repeatedly until the postal worker has collected all the mail. Then repeatedly sing the second verse of the song as he passes each child a piece of mail. Have the postal carrier choose his replacement, and repeat the singing/mail-collecting process.

Postal Carrier's Song

(sung to the tune of "Oh Dear, What Can The Matter Be?")

Mailing a letter from me to you.
It needs a stamp. I think one will do.
Mailman, deliver my letter soon.
I like to send mail. Don't you?

Oh, here's a letter from you to me.
It has a stamp. Why, just look and see!
Mailman, it means so much to me.
I love to get mail. Don't you?

Envelope Placemats

While the mail may be moving smoothly in your postal neighborhood, it wouldn't be moving at all if it weren't for a prominent address on each piece of mail. Use this skill-building activity to emphasize the importance of addresses. Enlarge the envelope pattern (page 62) so that it nearly fills a regular sheet of paper. Program it with the return address of your school. Then duplicate a construction-paper copy for each of your students.

Working with each child individually or with small groups of children, review the attributes of envelopes. As a prompt, sing "I'm A Little Letter" (page 59) and look through mail samples together. Then have each child dictate his address to you. Invite each child to stamp his envelope with a sticky stamp (see page 58) or a previously used stamp, or to draw an original stamp design in the space provided. Laminate each student's envelope and use it as a placemat at snacktime. Not only will the placemats help children find their places at the table, but you can also use snacktime to slip in a little address practice.

Tip-Top Day Care
212 Nurture Street
Happy Town, USA

Geordie Marx
555 Seashore Lane
Happy Town, USA

Special Delivery To Parents

Just after each student has first used his placemat (see "Envelope Placemats") is a perfect time to drop a note to moms and dads. Make a copy of the parent postcard (page 62) for each student. Again have him dictate as much of his address as he can remember as you write it on his copy of the parent postcard. Have him select a sticky stamp (if you made stamps as described on page 58) and attach it in the correct location. To complete the postcard, have each child turn to the blank side of his card and draw a picture of a postal worker. Parents will be pleased to learn what their youngsters have been learning in school and are likely to help make a pleasing difference in your students' address memorization.

Dear Family,
I am learning all about sending mail. Did you know that every letter needs a stamp and an address?
Today I practiced [illegible]ying my address. [illegible]ease help me [illegible]ractice some more!
Kyla

Kyla
2020 Happy Dr.
Anytown, USA

Postage With Personality Plus

Before using the stamps on page 63 to make a sorting center, duplicate page 64 for later use. Cut the stamps apart, and attach each one to a different 5" x 7" index card. Program each card with a return address and a fictitious address for the storybook character shown on the stamp before laminating it. Store these imitation envelopes in a real mailbox. To use this center, have a youngster remove the envelopes from the mailbox and examine them. Have him decide which stamps may have been from the same commemorative story set and sort the mail accordingly. Encourage him to talk about how he arrived at his sorting conclusions, before returning the mail to the mailbox.

Goldilocks
123 Forest Lane
Bearboro, USA

Peter Pig
24-B Twig Road
Blowtown, USA

Party At The Classroom Post Office

Read aloud *A Letter To Amy* by Ezra Jack Keats (HarperCollins Children's Books). Talk about how the boy got the party invitation. Explain to your children that in celebration of all their postal work, your class will be having a party. (If you care to time the postal party so that it can also be used as a valentine exchange, your celebration will be all the more festive!) Encourage each student to dictate (or write) an invitation for his family. Before sealing these letters inside envelopes, slip in copies of a full explanation, giving parents all the necessary details about the celebration. (In this note, you may want to ask each parent to bring along a special letter or card—and its envelope—that was sent to her in the mail.) Have each student help you recall his home address as you write it on the envelope. Let him use a school stamp and stamp pad to put the return address on the envelope, and have him attach the proper postage. Take all your students to a mail collection box and have them drop the invitations inside.

Before the big day arrives, solicit the help of a parent volunteer to make a sheet cake that resembles an addressed envelope for the party. Ask another volunteer to make a tape of songs that have a postal theme (such as "Return To Sender" and "Please, Mr. Postman"). Before parents arrive, have students don their postal badges (page 57), and begin to play your specially prepared tape. When the guests have arrived, have students guide tours of their classroom post office. Later while everyone is enjoying a slice of the cake, give parents an opportunity to show students special letters that they have brought with them or tell about special letters they have received. When it's time for the party to wind down, send parents off by having your students sing a rousing rendition of "I'm A Little Letter" (page 59).

Mrs. Lacher's Class
Kids' Place Center
Happytown, USA

First-Class Reading

The Jolly Postman Or Other People's Letters
Written by Janet & Allan Ahlberg
Published by Little, Brown and Company

Richard Scarry's Postman Pig And His Busy Neighbors
Written by Richard Scarry
Published by Random House, Inc.

Mr. Griggs' Work
Written by Cynthia Rylant
Published by Orchard Books

Dear Annie
Written by Judith Caseley
Published by Mulberry Books

Love, Your Bear Pete
Written by Dyan Sheldon
Published by Candlewick Press

Envelope Pattern

Use with "Up Close And Personal" on page 56, "A Classy Post Office" on page 57, and "Envelope Placemats" on page 60.

Parent Postcard

Use with "Special Delivery To Parents" on page 60.

Dear Family,

I am learning all about sending mail. Did you know that every letter needs a stamp and an address?

Today I practiced saying my address. Please help me practice some more!

Commemorative Story Stamps

Use with "Postage With Personality Plus" on page 60.

Goldilocks
&
The Three Bears

The Three
Billy Goats Gruff

The Three
Little Pigs

The Little
Red Hen

Postal Workers' Badge Patterns

Use with "Uniforms For All" on page 57, "Moving The Mail To A Beat" on page 59, and "Party At The Classroom Post Office" on page 61.

Mailbox Flags

Use with "Maiboxes" on page 58.

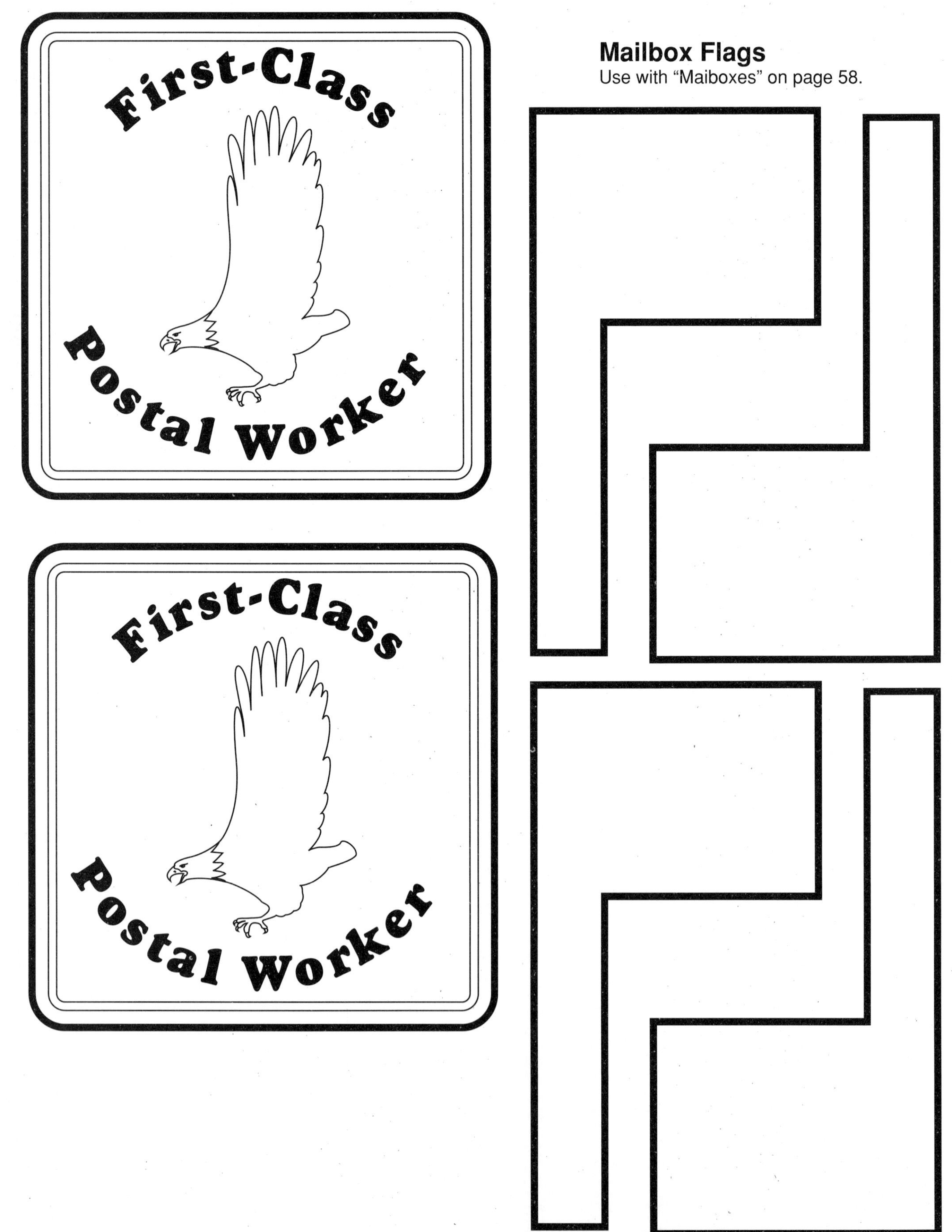

Classroom Post Office Logo

Use with "A Classy Post Office" on page 57 and "Mailboxes" on page 58.

You've Got To Have Heart!

It's not really the shape of a valentine, nor is it located on the left side of the chest. Instead it looks like an upside-down pear and only *tilts* to the left from its position in the middle of the chest. What is it? The heart! Entice your students to some creative scientific exploration with these heartwarming activities during the month of February—American Heart Month.

ideas contributed by Suzanne Moore

I Have A Pump

Get the minds of your youngsters a-thumping with this verse on the heart a-pumping! But first explain to youngsters that a pump is a device that is pressed in some way so that it moves substances—such as water—from one place to another. Ask students to name any pumps they might be familiar with—or give them examples—such as a gas, water, or liquid-soap pump. Then tell students that they each have a special pump inside their own bodies. Encourage youngsters to brainstorm what they think their special pumps might be. After students arrive at the correct answer—the heart, teach them this verse and the accompanying actions.

My Pump

I have a pump inside of me. *(Point to chest.)*
It works all night and day. *(Open and close fist.)*

My pump starts going really fast *(Open and close fist faster.)*
When I go out and play! *(Move arms as if running.)*

My pump slows down inside of me *(Open and close fist slower.)*
When I lay down and rest. *(Lay cheek against folded hands.)*

I know my pump and where it is— *(Point to temple.)*
My heart! Here in my chest! *(Point to chest.)*

Pumping Action

Students will develop a better understanding of the pumping action of the heart when they try this experiment. Explain that the heart acts like a pump by squeezing the blood from the heart into the arteries. Then invite students to perform firsthand pumping using a simulated pump to represent the heart—such as a bulb syringe, a baby bottle with a nipple, or even a squeeze bottle of tempera paint. Provide a student with an empty container and a liquid-filled pump simulator. Ask him to squeeze the pump so that the liquid squirts into the container. Point out that his squeezing causes the liquid to move from the pump to the container—just as the heart squeezes blood into the arteries. After each child has had a turn squeezing the pump, invite small groups of students to take turns experimenting with a variety of squeeze bottles and containers in a partially filled water table.

A Hard Worker

Do your students know which of their muscles is the hardest worker? After making these comparisons, they'll surely agree that the heart is! Ask students to find one of their muscles. Most likely they will flex their biceps. Then invite them to put that muscle to work by exercising it. Have the students repeatedly raise and lower their arms for a full minute. After the minute, ask students how their arms feel. Are they tired? Do they need to rest? If students appear to have the energy, have them repeat the exercise, this time for two minutes. Now how do their arms feel? If desired, also have students use their leg muscles by running in place until they tire. Then explain that when our muscles—such as those in the arms or legs—are used continuously, they eventually tire and must stop to rest. The heart, however, continues to beat *all* the time, *never* stopping nor resting—it's the hardest working muscle in the body!

The Size Of My Heart

What can youngsters learn by making a fist? They can learn about the sizes of their hearts! To prepare for this activity, put one 12-inch length of red yarn, one 12-inch length of blue yarn, and a copy of the parent letter on page 72 in a resealable plastic bag for each child. Then invite each youngster to make a fist and hold it in front of her. Explain that the heart is about the same size as a person's fist. Have each child place her fist against the middle of her chest to demonstrate just how large her heart is in comparison to her body. Then encourage her to take home a prepared bag to complete the enclosed activity with her parent.

After each child returns her bag, remove each yarn length and attach it to a red, construction-paper heart cutout labeled with the appropriate person's name. Have each child compare her yarn length to that of her parent's. Which person does she think has the larger heart? Explain that the larger a person's fist, the larger is her heart.

For an additional challenge, have each child look around the classroom for an object that is similar in size to her fist. Then have her use her yarn length to measure around the object to compare the actual circumference of her fist to that of the object. If desired, have her also try to find an object similar in size to her parent's heart. After making the observations and comparisons in this activity, each youngster will be proud to tell you about her big heart.

Dear Parent,

Our class is learning all kinds of interesting information about the heart! Did you know that a person's fist is about the size of his heart? Please share this bit of information with your child. Then follow the directions using the two lengths of yarn in this bag to measure both your own and your child's fists. Please enclose and return the lengths of yarn in this bag to school on _______________ (date). We will use these yarn lengths in a classroom measurement activity.

Directions:

1. Make a fist.
2. Tape one end of the blue yarn to the thumb side of your hand. Wrap the yarn around your knuckles and back around to your thumb.
3. Cut the yarn where it meets the other end.
4. Remove the yarn from your hand; then remove the tape from the yarn.
5. Place the yarn in the bag.
6. Repeat the procedure, using the red yarn to measure your child's fist.

Thank you for participating in your child's learning!

_______________________ (teacher)

Now Hear This!

Invite youngsters to a hearty session of listening to heart sounds when they use these various types of stethoscopes. In advance duplicate a class quantity of the parent request letter on page 72; then send a copy of the letter home with each student. After students bring the donated items to school, guide individuals or small groups to create some of the stethoscopes described.

One-Ear Models

The first stethoscope was a monaural (one-ear) hollow, wooden tube. The user of this stethoscope would place the tube against the patient's chest, then listen to the heart through a carved earpiece that fit into one ear. Have students make and use some of these one-ear stethoscope models from the suggested items.

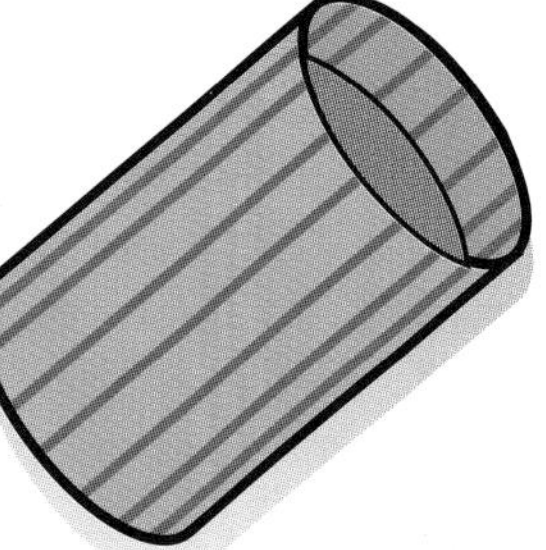

- Cardboard tubes: Have youngsters cover toilet-tissue or paper-towel tubes with adhesive-backed vinyl fabric or Con-Tact® covering.
- Paper cups: Help each student remove the bottom from a paper cup; then have him listen to the heart through the narrow end of the cup.
- Cans: For each student or group of students, remove both ends from a can; then cover both rims with vinyl tape. Have the student decorate a piece of construction paper cut to fit around the can. Then have him glue the paper around the can. After the glue dries, encourage him to use his metal tube as a stethoscope.
- Funnels: For each child or group of children, obtain a plastic funnel or create one by cutting off the top of a one-liter plastic soda bottle and covering the cut edge with vinyl tape. Have the student listen to a heart through the narrow end of the funnel.

Two-Ear Models

The two-ear, or *binaural*, stethoscope was designed in the early 1900s. Invite youngsters to use these stethoscopes to listen to a heart; then encourage them to compare the quality of the sound with that heard through a one-ear model of a stethoscope. As each student completes his turn using a two-ear stethoscope, use a cotton ball dipped in alcohol to sterilize the earpieces before having another student put them in his ears.

- Toy stethoscopes: Obtain several realistic toy stethoscopes from toy doctor kits. Have students use these to listen to each other's hearts.
- Funnel and rubber tubing: Create a large model of a stethoscope by attaching one end of a 12-inch length of rubber tubing to the narrow end of a plastic funnel; then attach a three-way tube connector (available at most hardware stores) to the other end of the rubber tube. Attach a separate 12-inch length of hose to each remaining end of the tube connector to complete the stethoscope. Invite students in turn to use this large stethoscope.
- Real stethoscopes: Purchase or borrow a real stethoscope for youngsters to use.

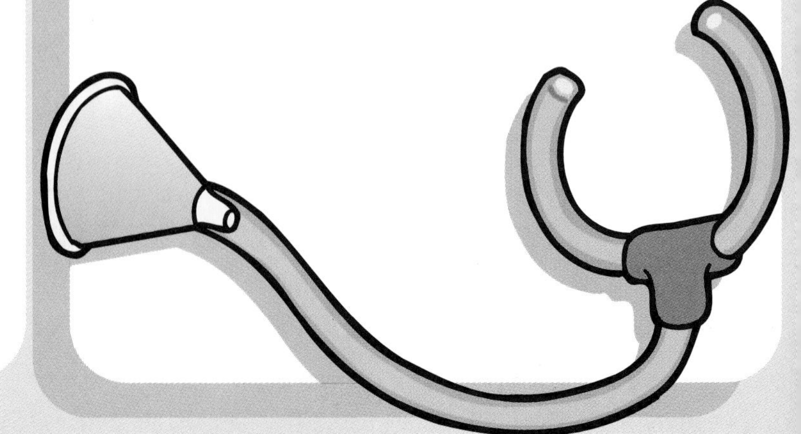

Heart Sounds

Ask students to describe the sound of a heartbeat and you'll most likely get a variety of responses. A heart's beat might be referred to as thumping, beating, drumming, and pounding, while the sound it makes might have many descriptors such as thump-thump, ba-bump, da-dum, and flub-dub. Explain to students that a valve in the heart opens and closes to let blood pass through. The movement of this valve causes the heart to make a sound—similar to a door that is opened and closed. Then teach youngsters this rhythmic chant to recite while they jump rope or jump into and out of large plastic rings placed on the floor.

Flub-dub

Flub-dub, flub-dub, goes my heart.
I listen to its beat.
It's pushing blood through my veins and lungs.
From my head down to my feet.

Flub-dub, flub-dub, goes my heart.
It's working like a pump.
Each time it beats, it pumps my blood,
When I sleep and walk and JUMP!

Speed It Up

Throbbing hearts and racing pulses will result after little ones participate in this game requiring quick ears and feet. Take your class to a gym or outdoor field. Before beginning this activity, guide each student to place a hand on the middle of his chest to feel his heart beat. Does he think his heart is beating fast or slow? Then instruct the students to listen for your directions to "Walk," "Jump," or "Run." As they hear each direction, have them perform that action until another action is named. Then have them immediately perform the next action. Encourage youngsters to listen carefully as you randomly give the directions, sometimes naming two actions in quick succession. After a vigorous two to three minutes of listening and moving, have each student stop and feel his heart again. Is it beating fast or slow? Did it speed up?

After a short rest period, help each student locate his pulse at his wrist. Ask the students to check their pulses to see how fast their hearts are beating. How fast do their pulses feel now? Then invite students to repeat the movement activity, this time checking and commenting on their pulse rates after they stop their movement. What did they learn? That quick ears and fast feet make a speedy heart!

Pulse Spots

Youngsters will easily be able to locate some of their pulse points as well as learn some body parts with this song. To begin, help each child place two fingers on one side of his neck to locate his pulse. When he finds his pulse, have him place a sticker dot on that location so that he can quickly find his pulse again. In the same fashion, help him locate and mark his pulse at his wrist, temple, and ankle. Then have him touch each pulse spot as it is mentioned in this song. For additional fun, have the students repeat the song several times, each time a little faster than the time before. After the last verse, encourage each child to choose one spot at which to check his pulse rate. Encourage students to comment on the rates of their pulses.

(sung to the tune of "Head, Shoulders, Knees, And Toes")

Head and neck,
And wrist and ankle.
Wrist and ankle.

Head and neck,
And wrist and ankle.
Wrist and ankle.

I can find my pulse
At all of these spots.

At my head and neck,
And wrist and ankle.
Wrist and ankle.

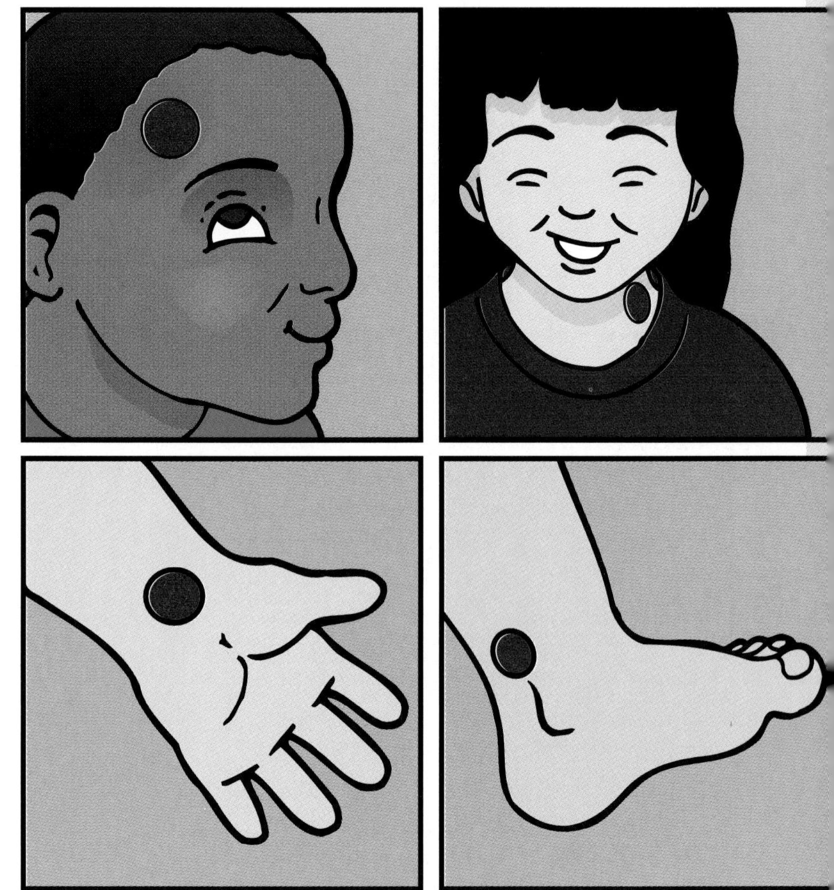

Now that youngsters know where their pulses can be felt, invite them to periodically check their pulses after different activities during the routine of their day. Ask them to compare their pulse rates after activities such as resting, playing with blocks, and running outdoors. After which activities do their pulses beat the fastest?

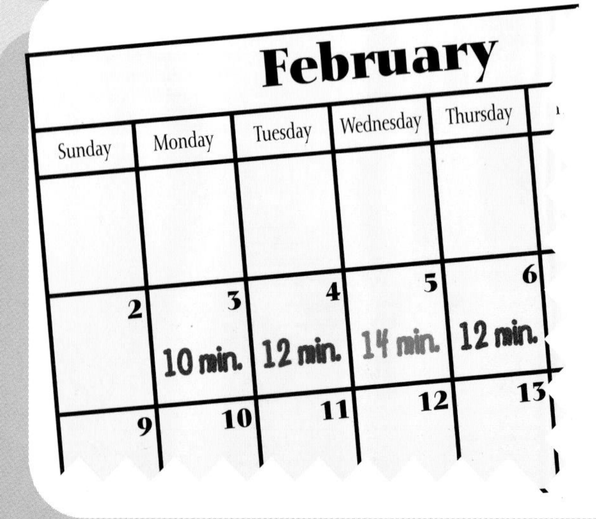

Walk The Talk!

Emphasize the contribution that exercise makes in having a healthy heart by involving students in some healthy exercise. Tell youngsters that when they exercise, their hearts beat faster and pump more oxygen-rich blood to their muscles. Exercise helps keep their hearts and bodies healthy. Then follow up the talk by doing the walk! Each day for a week, take your class on a walk around the school campus or other designated area. Record the amount of time the class walks each day on a calendar. At the end of the week, total the amount of walk time taken that week. Commend students on participating in a heart-healthy exercise, and encourage them to continue to exercise in heart-smart ways.

Good For Your Heart

This tasty, heartwarming treat will provide youngsters with a good example of a snack that is healthy for the heart. Inform students that, in addition to exercise, another way to keep their hearts healthy is to eat healthy meals and snacks. Ask them to brainstorm a list of some snacks they think are healthy for their hearts. Write their responses on a heart-shaped construction-paper cutout. Display the cutout with the title "Good For Your Heart." Then invite youngsters to help make some good-for-your-heart pretzels with this recipe.

Good-For-Your-Heart Pretzels

2 packages yeast
1 1/2 cups warm water
1 tsp. salt
2 Tbsp. sugar
4 cups flour
1 egg, beaten
salt

Preheat the oven to 425˚F. Mix the yeast and water in a large bowl; then mix in the salt, sugar, and flour. Turn the dough out onto a sheet of waxed paper. Knead the dough until it is smooth and elastic. Roll pieces of the dough into snakes; then shape the snakes into heart shapes on a greased cookie sheet. Let the dough hearts rise until they double in size; then brush some of the beaten egg onto each heart pretzel. Sprinkle each pretzel sparingly with salt. Bake them for 15 minutes or until golden brown. Cool and serve.

Smart About My Heart

Invite youngsters to create these heart-smart booklets to summarize some of the things they have learned about their hearts. For each child, duplicate the booklet cover and pages on pages 73–75 on white construction paper. Have each student cut apart his booklet pages and stack them in sequence behind his booklet cover; then staple the pages together along the left edge. Encourage each child to follow the provided directions to complete each page. Then invite youngsters to take their booklets home to share with their families.

- Booklet cover: Instruct the student to glue a small photograph (or duplicated photo) at the tail of the speech bubble, then write his name on the line.
- Page 1: Have the student trace around his fist and color in the resulting form.
- Page 2: Ask the student to color the picture. Have him glue a fabric rectangle over the child's body to represent a blanket.
- Page 3: Encourage the child to color the picture; then have him glue a few small, construction-paper shape cutouts on the page to represent blocks.
- Page 4: Have the student color the picture; then help him glue a length of yarn arcing over the child's head with each yarn end in one of the child's hands so that it represents a jump rope.
- Page 5: Invite the child to draw one of his favorite healthy foods on the plate. Or have him glue a magazine cutout of the food on the plate. Write the food name on the line.

Letter To Parent

Use with "The Size Of My Heart" on page 67.

Dear Parent,

Our class is learning all kinds of interesting information about the heart! Did you know that a person's fist is about the size of his heart? Please share this bit of information with your child. Then follow the directions using the two lengths of yarn in this bag to measure both your own and your child's fists. Please enclose and return the lengths of yarn in this bag to school on ________________. We will use these yarn lengths in a classroom measurement activity. (date)

Directions:

1. Make a fist.
2. Tape one end of the blue yarn to the thumb side of your hand. Wrap the yarn around your knuckles and back around to your thumb.
3. Cut the yarn where it meets the other end.
4. Remove the yarn from your hand; then remove the tape from the yarn.
5. Place the yarn in the bag.
6. Repeat the procedure, using the red yarn to measure your child's fist.

Thank you for participating in your child's learning!

____
(teacher)

Parent Request Letter

Use with "Now Hear This!" on page 68.

Dear Parent,

During our study of the heart, we will be making stethoscopes from a variety of materials. In order to stock our classroom for this project, we need a supply of the items listed below. Please donate any items that you can. We would appreciate receiving any recycled items empty and clean! Send the items to school by ________.
(date)

cardboard tubes (toilet-tissue or paper-towel tubes)
paper cups (9-ounce size preferred)
16-ounce cans (preferably with both ends removed)
one-liter soda bottles
plastic funnels
rubber tubing

Also, if you have a real or toy stethoscope that our class may borrow, please label it with your child's name and send it with your donated items.

Thank you for supporting our class!

____
(teacher)

I'm Smart
About
My Heart
by
My heart is about this big.
1

Booklet Pages
Use with "Smart About My Heart" on page 71.

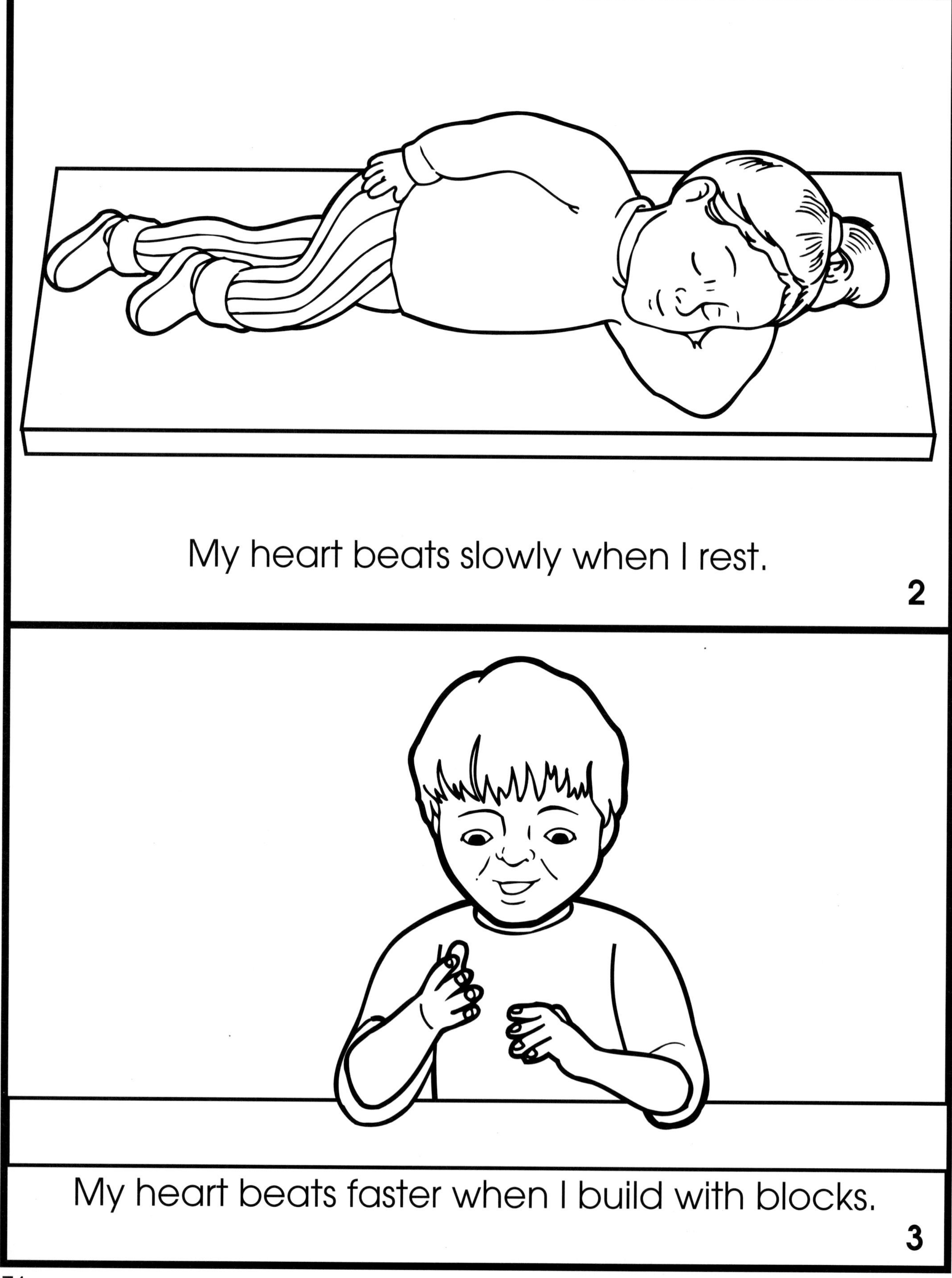

Use with "Smart About My Heart" on page 71.

We Are Alike And Different

The activities in this unit will help you explore the concepts of *alike* and *different* with your youngsters. Begin by focusing on objects; then expand your comparisons to include people. Help little ones understand that while all people share basic physical characteristics and needs, each of us is a unique individual in the way she looks, acts, thinks, and feels.

ideas contributed by Ada Hanley Goren and Lucia Kemp Henry

Alike And Different

Introduce the concepts of alike and different with this poem and some construction-paper shapes. Before sharing the verse, cut two small, red circles and a large, blue square from construction paper. As you recite the first verse, hold up the two red circles and invite youngsters to comment on how the two cutouts are alike. Youngsters may point out the size, shape, color, or material of the cutouts. As you recite the second verse, hold up one of the red circles and the blue square. Invite the students to cite differences in the two cutouts. Again guide the children to mention the sizes, shapes, and colors of the cutouts.

Verse 1:

Things can be so much alike.
Things can be the same.
Things can have a similar shape,
Or look, or sound, or name.

These things are so much alike.
These things are the same.
What makes these things so much alike?
What likenesses can you name?

Verse 2:

Things can be quite different.
Some things are not the same.
Things can have a different shape,
Or look, or sound, or name.

These things are quite different.
These things are not the same.
What makes these things so different?
What differences can you name?

Shape Up And Sort Out

This shape-sorting activity will further clarify the meanings of *alike* and *different.* In advance prepare a set of construction-paper shapes. Cut three red circles that exactly match the red circles used in "Alike And Different" on page 76 (for a total of five red circles), as well as a red square, a red heart, a red star, and a red triangle. Make all these shapes similar in size. Then label two sheets of tagboard—one with the word "Alike" and one with the word "Different."

Gather a small group of youngsters around a table. Present the set of shapes; then ask the children to find the shapes that are alike. Have them place those shapes on the sheet of tagboard labeled "Alike." Have the children place the remaining shapes on the tagboard sheet labeled "Different." Ask the children to verbalize their reasoning as they work. Some youngsters may reason that all the shapes are alike because they are made of paper and they are red. Acknowledge these similarities before directing the children's attention to the shape differences.

Whose Shoes?

Extend youngsters' skills with identifying likenesses and differences when you play this fun footwear matching game. Have students sit in a circle, with their feet in front of them and the bottoms of their shoes on the floor. Invite one child to stand and find a pair of shoes that are like his shoes in some way. Have him tell how the two pairs of shoes are alike (shoelaces, color, material, etc.) Then have the child whose shoes were chosen stand and find a pair of shoes that are like hers in some way. Continue in this manner for several rounds. Then change the game by asking a child to identify a pair of shoes that are different from hers in some way. Continue play with this new twist for a few rounds, giving every child an opportunity to participate. Bet you never knew there was so much to say about shoes!

The Same Song

For this activity, gather several pairs of objects. Each pair should share at least one common characteristic. For example, collect two types of fruit, two stuffed animals, and two writing utensils. Then teach your youngsters this song, sung to the tune of "The Farmer In The Dell." Each time they sing the song, hold up a pair of objects and ask student volunteers to describe how the items are alike. Then have youngsters talk about the differences in the pair of objects.

Oh, how are they alike?
Oh, how are they alike?
Oh, oh, do you know just how they are alike?

Once your little ones can find likenesses and differences in objects, focus their attention on likenesses and differences in people. Ask a pair of students to stand in front of the group as the song is sung. Then have student volunteers cite likenesses and differences between the two children. Guide children to notice hair color or texture, height, and clothing differences. Repeat the song until each child has had a turn to stand in front of the group.

Look. We have sneakers that are alike!

People Are Alike And Different

Share this poem with your little ones to help them focus on likenesses and differences among people.

People are alike and different, too—
People like you and me.
Some things can make us different and
Some things are the same, you see.

People are alike 'cause they have eyes—
People like you and me.
Some eyes are brown, some blue, some green.
Some people wear glasses to see.

People are alike 'cause they have skin—
People like you and me.
Some skin is light, some dark, some tan,
The colors don't matter, you see!

People are alike 'cause they have homes—
People like you and me.
A home can be a house or a tent
Or a boat on the deep blue sea.

People are alike 'cause they need food—
People like you and me.
We all have tastes for different foods,
Like tacos or pasta or peas!

People are alike 'cause they need love—
People like you and me.
All people need love to thrive and grow
To feel happy and safe and free!

Face To Face

Expand upon the ideas in the poem "People Are Alike And Different" by discussing likenesses and differences in facial features. Read *Two Eyes, A Nose, And A Mouth* by Roberta Grobel Intrater (Scholastic Inc.). This book's simple text points out that while we all share the same basic facial features, each of us has a unique face. It also celebrates our differences and notes that the world would be a pretty boring place if everyone looked exactly the same!

After sharing the book, make a display to celebrate the unique faces of your youngsters. Use an instant camera to take a close-up picture of each student's face. Then mount all the pictures on a bulletin board in several rows (similar to some of the book's illustrations). Add a title that reads "Two Eyes, A Nose, And A Mouth, You See—But Each As Different As Different Can Be!"

Tastes Differ

Besides physical characteristics, how else are we alike, yet different? Pose this question to your youngsters and discuss their responses. Reread the poem "People Are Alike And Different" to stimulate children's thinking. Then expand on one idea mentioned in the poem—foods—with this alike-and-different game.

In advance help each youngster put together an ice-cream-cone necklace. For each child provide a light brown, construction-paper cone cutout. Invite each child to select a construction-paper scoop cutout to represent the flavor of ice cream she prefers—brown for chocolate, pink for strawberry, or white for vanilla. Then have her glue her scoop to her cone. Assist her in punching a hole in the top of the scoop, threading a length of yarn through the hole, and tying the yarn ends together to create a necklace. Have each child wear her necklace.

Begin the activity by having the children say, "We are alike because we like ice cream!" Then say, "Chocolate, vanilla, strawberry, too. Who likes the same kind of ice cream as you?" Ask each youngster to find and hold hands with at least one person wearing the same kind of necklace as she is wearing. For the next round of play, say, "Chocolate, vanilla, strawberry, too. Who likes a different kind of ice cream than you?" Then ask each child to find and hold hands with at least one person who is wearing a *different* kind of necklace. Continue for several rounds, alternating between like and unlike pairings of necklaces.

Books About Diversity

Share one of these selections for further discussion about the likenesses and differences among people of the world.

We Are All Alike...We Are All Different
Written by The Cheltenham Elementary School Kindergartners
Published by Scholastic Inc.

Children Just Like Me
Written by Barnabas and Anabel Kindersley
Published by Dorling Kindersley

Charles Simpson and Frankie Foster

We are alike because we are boys. We both like scary movies and we both have brown hair.

We are different because Charles has a brother and Frankie has two sisters. Charles live in Wallburg and Frankie lives in Graham.

Compare The Pair

Conclude your study by creating a class book that compares likenesses and differences in your students. Ask each child to find a partner. Have the student pair pose for an instant photo. Then duplicate a copy of page 80 for each pair to complete.

Ask the students to dictate things that they have in common and ways they differ. After writing their dictation, glue the photo of the pair to the page. Mount each page on a sheet of construction paper; then bind all the pages between construction-paper covers. Write the title "Compare The Pairs" on the book cover and add it to your classroom library for youngsters to enjoy.

_______________ and _______________

(student name) (student name)

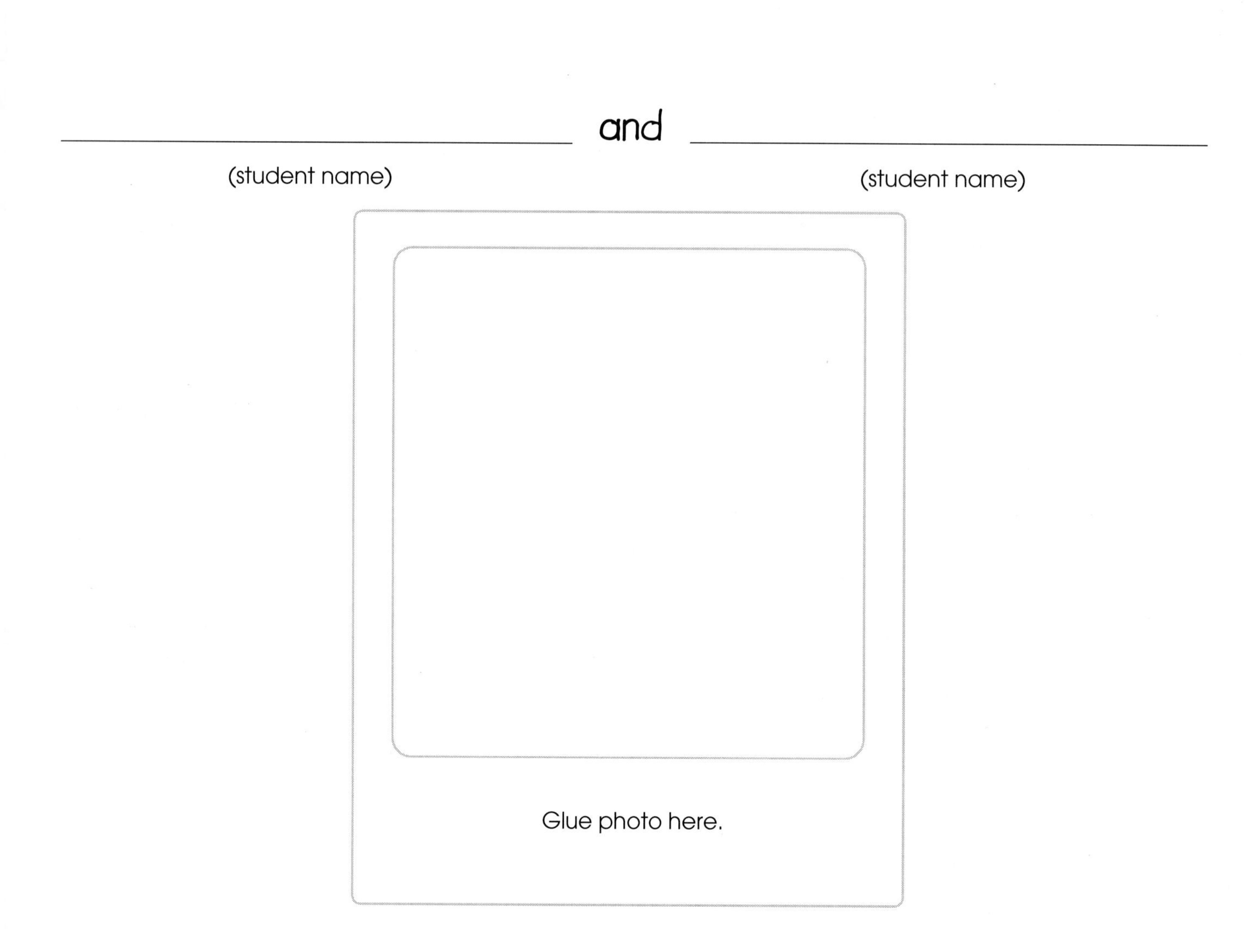

We are alike because _______________________________

____.

We are different because ____________________________

____.

 Note To The Teacher: Use with “Compare The Pair” on page 79.

Hip, Hip, Hooray! It's The 100th Day!

If you and your kindergartners have been keeping track of the school days since the beginning of the year, it's time to celebrate a mathematical milestone—the 100th day of school! Use these activities to help your young learners grasp the concept of "100." One hundred days of school? Cool!

ideas contributed by Ada Hanley Goren and Vicki Pacchetti

Dressed For The Occasion

You can count on this sweatshirt to be the perfect attire for your 100th Day activities—and your students can count on it, too! Before the 100th day of school, purchase an oversized, solid-colored sweatshirt, two shades of fabric paint, and 100 pom-poms (preferably ten each of ten different colors). Beginning at one shoulder, use hot glue or fabric glue to attach the pom-poms (like colors together) in a line that wraps around and around the shirt until all the pom-poms have been used. After the glue dries, use one shade of fabric paint to write the numeral "1" below the first pom-pom. Continue labeling each pom-pom in numerical order, switching to the other paint color to write each numeral divisible by ten (10, 20, 30, etc.). Wear the finished sweatshirt as part of your 100th Day celebration.

Count On It!

A study of the number 100 naturally lends itself to practice with counting—especially counting by tens. For this activity, you'll need several copies of the counting chart on page 85. First make one copy of the chart. Beginning with the numeral 1 in the top left corner, write the numerals 1–100 in the boxes. Make an enlarged copy of this chart to use with the whole class. Then duplicate a class supply of the numbered chart on colored paper. Finally duplicate a class supply of the original, blank chart on white copy paper. Cut the colored-paper copies into strips as shown. Leave the blank charts intact.

Show the students the enlarged chart. Review the numbers 1–100. Point out the numbers divisible by ten; then ask youngsters to look for other number patterns on the chart. As a class, practice counting aloud to 100, first by ones, then by tens. Point to each number on the chart as it is recited. Then give each child a blank chart, a set of number strips, and a glue stick. Ask him to glue the strips onto the counting chart in the correct order. When he has finished, have him refer to the enlarged chart to check his work.

100 Autographs

This cooperative activity will help you create a visual display of the number 100. Precut 100 strips of paper—ten each in ten different colors. Divide the slips as evenly as possible among your youngsters. Instruct each child to write her name on one of her slips; then ask her to collect a signature from someone at school—the principal, teachers, custodians, cafeteria workers, parent volunteers, or other students—on each of her remaining slips of paper. Send a parent volunteer or teacher's aide with small groups of signature seekers until each student has accomplished her mission. Once the slips of paper have been returned, have the children help you check to make sure all 100 slips of paper are accounted for. Instruct the children to sort the slips by color, then count together to be sure each pile contains ten slips. Divide a bulletin board into ten sections. Display the collected autographs—ten on each section of the board—with the title "Can You Count 100 Names?"

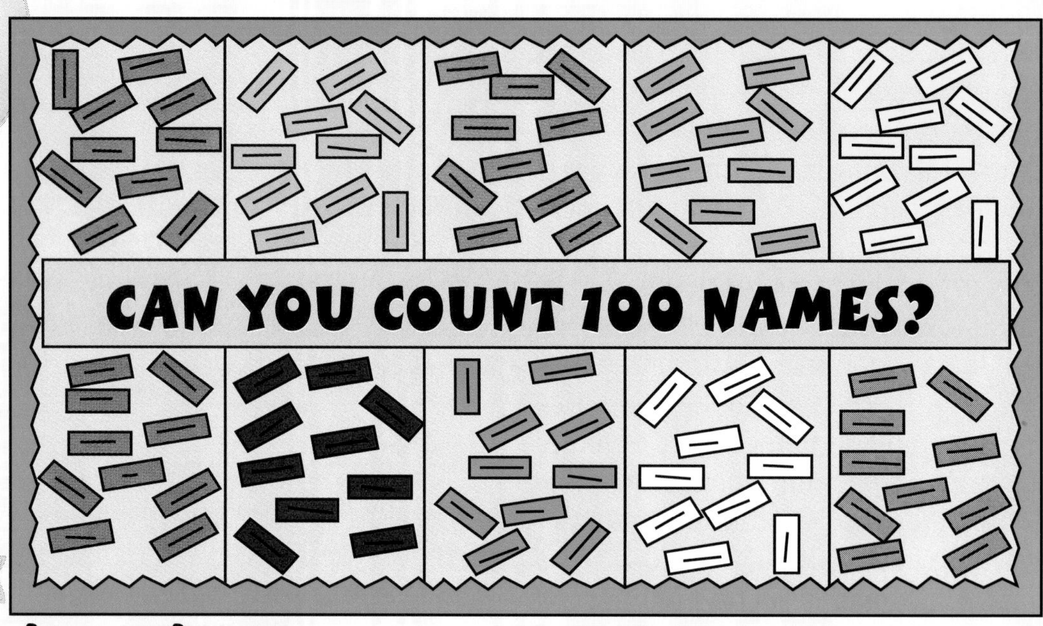

Currency Concepts

Youngsters are fascinated with the concept of 100, and they are even more fascinated with the concept of 100 *dollars.* Invite each child to describe what he might do with 100 dollars in this cute class book. To prepare pages for the book, first slightly enlarge, then photocopy a 100-dollar bill from a set of play money on green copy paper. Make enough copies to have one fake bill for each child. Cut out each fake bill; then cut out the center picture on each one. For each child's page, position a photocopy of that child's school picture at the center top edge of a sheet of white construction paper. Then glue the fake bill in place over the photocopied picture, so that the child's face shows through the opening in the bill. Encourage each child to illustrate—in the open space on his page—what he would do if he had 100 dollars. Write each child's dictation near his illustration. Stack the pages together and bind them between construction-paper covers. Write the title "If I Had A Hundred Dollars..." on the front cover. Place the book in the reading center for youngsters to read and enjoy.

100-Piece Creations

Provide a variety of manipulatives in quantities of 100 to get students involved in some creative, cooperative fun! Have youngsters help you count out 100 pattern blocks, 100 wooden blocks, or 100 pieces from any other suitable manipulative set in your classroom. Then divide the class into small groups and ask each group to take a turn creating a design or a structure using the 100 blocks or pieces. Take an instant photo of each group's finished project before inviting the next group to take its turn. Extend this activity by providing one or more 100-piece jigsaw puzzles for students to put together.

Take It Outside!

Take youngsters on a trip to the playground for some gross-motor experiences with the number 100. Lead the children in a variety of group activities, such as counting 100 trips down the slide, taking 100 steps from a designated point, or doing 100 jumping jacks. Finish off the outdoor fun with a 100-yard dash. Whew! Learning about 100 is exhausting!

Estimation Stations

Set up several estimation stations for math—100th Day style! If desired, divide your class into three groups and have the groups rotate from station to station.

Station One: Create three trains of plastic, snap-together cubes. Make one train exactly 100 cubes in length. Make each of the other two trains fewer than or more than 100 cubes in length. Invite each student to place his name card in a pile next to the train he believes to be exactly 100 cubes long. After everyone has estimated, count the cubes in each train to find out which one is made up of exactly 100 cubes. Read the name cards to identify the students who guessed correctly.

Station Two: Invite an adult volunteer to pose the question, "How long is 100 seconds?" Have her watch the clock and say, "Go!" when she begins her 100-second count. Direct each child to sit down when she thinks 100 seconds have passed. Have the volunteer ring a bell when 100 seconds have actually passed. Wow! 100 seconds is longer than you think!

Station Three: Collect five same-size, lidded jars. Place a different filler—such as peanuts, paper clips, cotton balls, M&M's®, and buttons—into each jar, filling one jar with exactly 100 items and putting fewer than or more than 100 items in each of the other jars. Place the lid on each jar; then glue a construction-paper square of a different color to each jar lid. Place the jars and a sheet of construction paper in each corresponding color on a tabletop. As students visit this station, have them examine the five jars and estimate which one contains exactly 100 items. Have each child write her name on the sheet of paper that corresponds to the jar-lid color of her choice. After everyone has made an estimate, count the contents of each jar together to determine which jar contains exactly 100 items. Then read and count the names on the paper to determine how many children guessed correctly.

100th Day Headbands

These headbands are right at your fingertips—or actually at your students' fingertips! Encourage each child to make 100 fingerprints to decorate a headband for your 100th Day celebration. For each child, cut a 3" x 24" strip of heavy white paper. Also cut a class supply—by hand or with a die-cutting machine—of the numeral 100 from brightly colored construction paper. Then purchase or borrow ten stamp pads in ten different colors.

Have each child glue his cutout numerals to the center of his white paper strip. Then have him press each of his fingers and thumbs—one at a time—onto a different stamp pad. On his white paper strip, have him make ten prints with each of his ten fingers. The result? 100 fancy fingerprints on one handsome headband! Fit each child's headband to his head and staple the ends together. All dressed? Let's celebrate!

A Colorful Counting Cake

What would a celebration be without a cake? Make this special cake in the shape of the number 100 to mark this very special school day. Have youngsters assist you in preparing the batter as directed on a package of cake mix. Divide the batter evenly among one square and two round cake pans. Bake the three cakes for approximately 25 minutes. Cool the cakes; then cut the square cake in half. Use one-half of the square cake as the number 1 and discard the other half. On a large tray or a sheet of cardboard covered with foil, place the square cake-half next to the two round cakes to form the number 100. Use canned cake frosting and decorator tube icing to delineate the numbers more clearly. Then have youngsters help you add the finishing touch—100 M&M's® candies! Invite each child to put on a few M&M's®; count together continuously until you reach 100. Encourage each youngster to enjoy a slice of this colorful counting cake as you share one of the stories listed in "Stories You Can Count On."

Stories You Can Count On

Extra! Extra! Read all about it—the number 100, that is! Share one or more of these just-right-for-the-100th-day-of-school stories with your little ones.

The Wolf's Chicken Stew
Written by Keiko Kasza
Published by G. P. Putnam's Sons

The 100th Day Of School
Written by Angela Shelf Medearis
Published by Scholastic Inc.

I Can Count To 100...Can You?
Written by Katherine Howard
Published by Random House, Inc.

Count To 100!

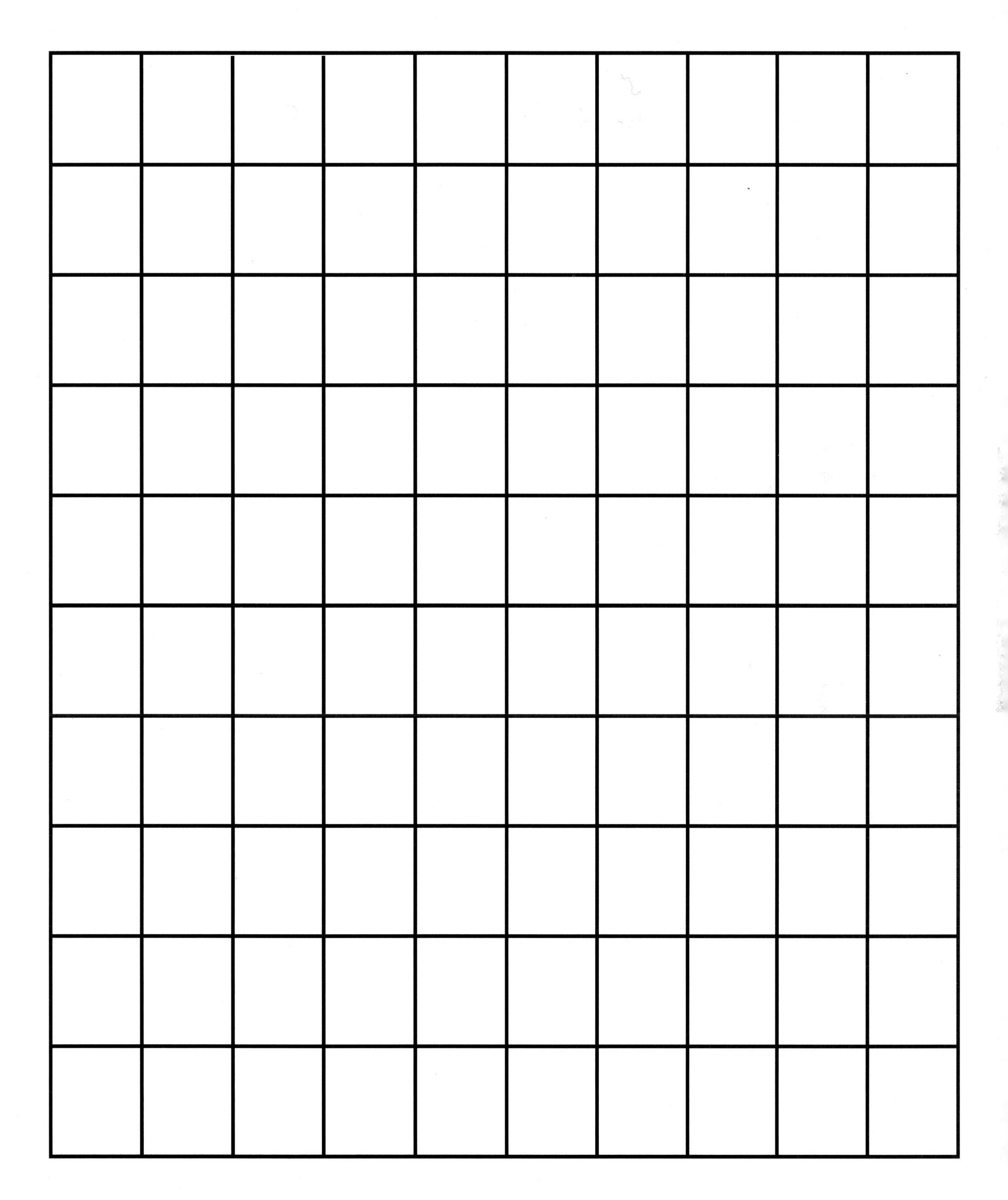

Note To The Teacher: Use with "Count On It!" on page 81.

The Wonderful World Of Whales

Plunge into the deep-sea world of these warm-blooded wonders and watch youngsters have a whale of a good time on their learning adventure.

ideas contributed by Lucia Kemp Henry

Those Cetacean Sensations!

Perk the curiosity of your youngsters by sharing some interesting facts about fascinating whales (see the fact box below). For visual aids, use illustrated reference books—such as A First Discovery Book: *Whales* (Scholastic Inc.) and Eyes On Nature: *Whales And Dolphins* by Anton Ericson (Kidsbooks Incorporated)—and the whale flannelboard figures on page 93.

Then invite each student to spout about what he has learned by dictating an interesting whale fact for you to write on a half-sheet of white construction paper. Draw a simple water-spout shape around each written statement; then have the child cut out the outline. Have each child glue his cutout to the top of a construction-paper whale cutout. Then display the fact-spouting whales with the title "Those Cetacean Sensations!"

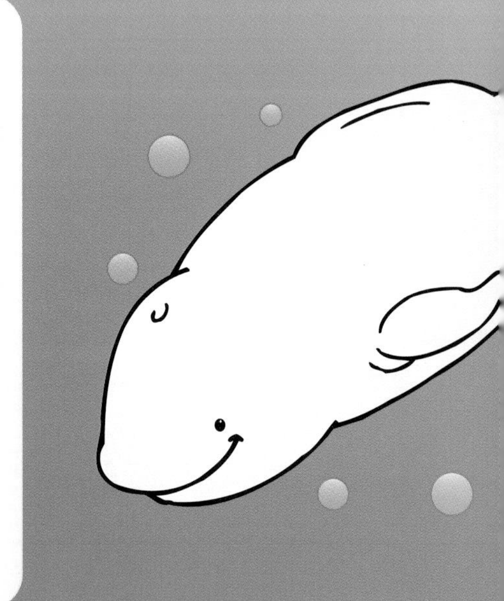

- Whales are similar to fish in many ways—they swim and hunt in the ocean and even resemble fish in appearance. But, unlike fish, whales have lungs and breathe air. A whale's body is covered with skin, not scales. Whale babies are born alive and drink milk from their mothers. All whales are warm-blooded—they are *mammals,* not fish.
- Whales belong to a family of mammals called *cetaceans* (see-TAY-shuns).
- Some whales—such as orcas, sperm whales, and belugas—have teeth with which they catch fish.
- Other whales—such as blue, humpback, and right whales—have comblike fibers in their mouths called *baleen.* Baleen are used to strain plankton—tiny sea creatures—from the seawater.
- All whales have two flippers and a tail called a *fluke.* A whale moves its fluke up and down to swim.
- Some whales have fins on their backs.
- Whales have *blowholes* (or nostrils) on the tops of their heads.
- Many whales live and travel in groups called *pods.*
- A male whale is called a *bull,* a female is a *cow,* and a young whale is a *calf.*
- Some whales *migrate*—or move—to warmer waters during the winter.

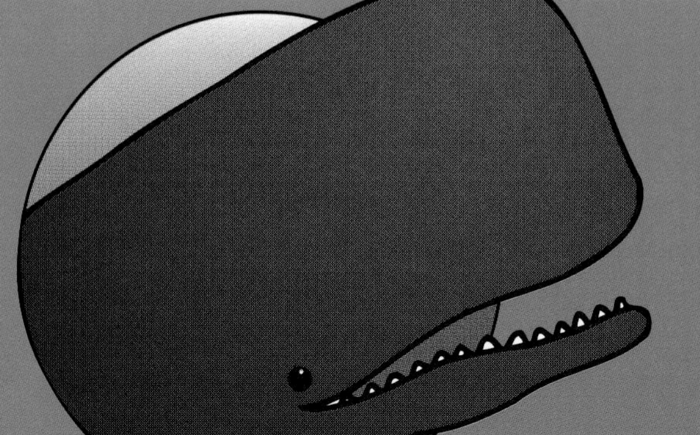

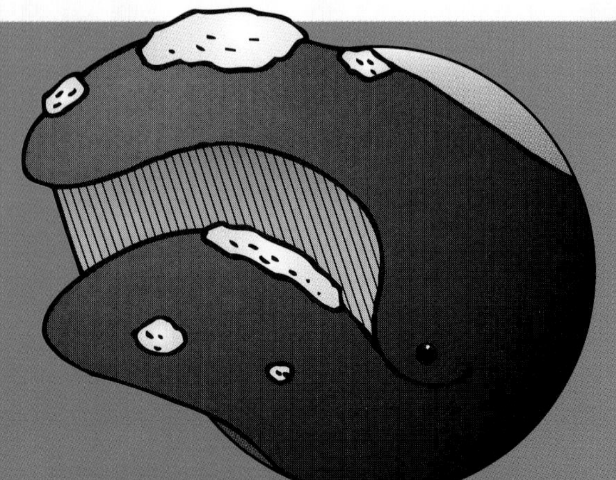

All Kinds Of Whales

It would be a huge order to ask youngsters to name all the different whales—there are 76 known types! But students can become familiar with a *few* different kinds of whales and build a whale of a vocabulary when they learn this flannelboard poem. In advance, copy page 94 for later use; then mount the whale flannelboard figures on page 93 on a sheet of tagboard. Cut out each figure and laminate it for durability. Attach the hook side of a piece of Velcro® to the back of each figure. As each verse is recited, place the corresponding figure on the board. Repeat the poem several times, each time inviting a different child to place the appropriate whale figure for each verse on the board.

All kinds of whales
Live in the salty sea.
They're not fish—but *mammals*
Just like you and me.

A *humpback* is giant.
Its *flippers* are so long.
It makes a special noise
That sounds just like a song.

A *gray whale* is huge.
Baleen fills its mouth.
When cold weather comes,
It *migrates* to the south.

An *orca* is large,
With black-and-white skin.
It has teeth so sharp
And a very tall *fin.*

A *beluga* is big.
Its skin—creamy white.
A *pod* of belugas
Is a beautiful sight!

A Whale Of A Book!

Youngsters will have a whale of a tale to share when they create these unique whale books. For each child, duplicate the whale head and tail book covers on page 92 and the book pages on pages 94 and 95 on white construction paper. Cut out several large and small whale shapes from sponges; then prepare several shallow trays of blue, black, or gray tempera paint. Have each child cut out his book covers and pages, then assemble his book as indicated. Ask the student to complete his book covers and pages as suggested. After the paint dries, help him accordion-fold the book pages so that only the whale's head and tail are visible. Encourage each child to take his book home to share with his family.

Book covers: Have the child color the whale's head and tail and write his name on the line.
Page 1: Have the student sponge-paint a whale. Have him color the page around the whale to resemble water.
Page 2: Have the child sponge-paint a large whale on the page. Invite him to glue a few strands of crinkled gift-wrap stuffing onto the whale's head to represent the spout.
Page 3: Encourage the child to sponge-paint a large and a small whale on the page.
Page 4: Have the child sponge-paint several whales on the page.

Puffy Whale Puppets

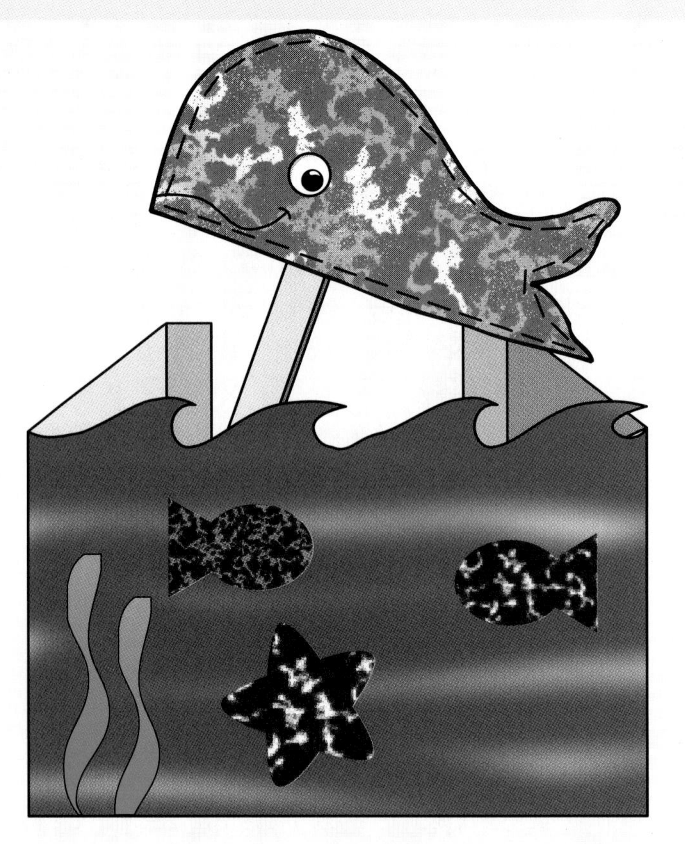

These cute cetacean puppets will be a big splash with youngsters in their dramatic play. To make a puppet, have a child sponge-paint a large sheet of newsprint with black, blue, gray, or white tempera paint, or any combination of the paints. After the paint dries, ask the student to fold her paper in half with the painted side out; then help her trace a simple whale shape on one side of her paper. Have her cut out the whale outline through both thicknesses of her paper. Staple the whale cutouts together along the edges, leaving an opening at the center bottom. Have the child draw a mouth and glue a wiggle eye onto each side of the whale. Then invite her to stuff the whale with crumpled pieces of tissue paper. Have the child insert the end of a wide craft stick into the opening and tape it in place. Then staple the edges together. Encourage youngsters to use their puffy whale puppets in their play activities as they share whale information with classmates.

A simple ocean-scene puppet stage can easily be made from a large box. Cut away the top and one side of a box. Trim the top of one side to resemble waves; then have small groups of youngsters take turns painting the box with blue tempera paint. After the paint dries, invite students to sponge-print sea creatures and glue strips of crepe-paper seaweed onto the box. Encourage students to take turns swimming their whale puppets around in the deep blue sea.

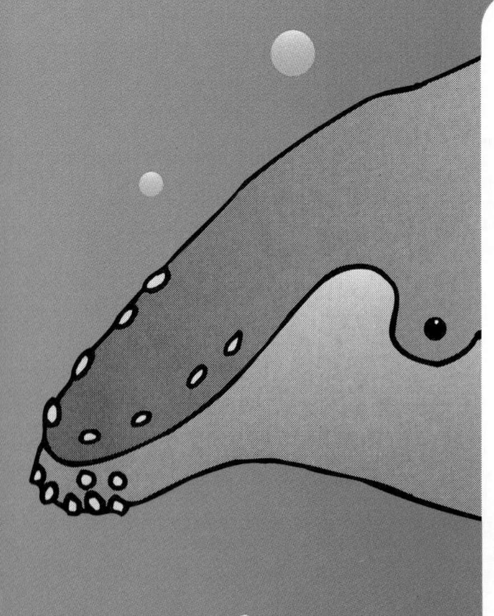

Seagoing Whales

Round up a pod of little whale puppeteers and invite them to move, swim, and dive their puppets (made in "Puffy Whale Puppets") to correspond to the words in this song.

A Whale Swims

(sung to the tune of "My Bonnie")

A whale swims around in the ocean.
A whale dives down deep in the sea.
A whale makes his home in the ocean.
A whale is much bigger than me!

Whales jump! Whales dive!
Whales swim around in the sea, the sea.
Whales splash! Whales spout!
And whales are much bigger than me!

Whales are...
huge
gigantic
jumbo
large

A Whopper Of A Whale!

This enlarged model of a whale will help little ones understand just how big a whale can be. Using an opaque projector, enlarge the flannelboard figure of the orca whale on page 93 onto a large canvas of pieced-together bulletin-board paper lengths so that the figure is between 20 and 30 feet in length. Cut out the whale along the resulting outline; then place the cutout on the floor in a large, cleared area of your classroom or a hallway. Invite small groups of youngsters to take turns sponge-painting the top portion of the orca whale with black tempera paint. After the paint dries, display the whale on a wall in your classroom or the hallway. Have youngsters use a variety of measuring devices—such as rulers, yardsticks, their arms, or even their body lengths—to measure the length of this whopping whale.

A Whale-Sized Vocabulary

The vocabulary of your youngsters will grow to epic proportions when they learn different words to describe the size of a whale. Explain to students that the word *big* is used to describe the size of whales, but it doesn't seem to convey their truly stupendous, enormous, humongous sizes! Then invite youngsters to brainstorm other words that mean the same as or are extensions of the word *big.* Record their responses on a white, spout-shaped, bulletin-board cutout programmed with "Whales are...." Display the cutout above the whale created in "A Whopper Of A Whale!"

A Salty Whale Chanty

Invite little ones to don the role of seafarers as they recite this counting poem in sailor fashion. Have a volunteer place a whale figure from page 93 on the flannelboard for each verse. Encourage the other students to perform the accompanying movements to each line. Repeat the second verse two times, replacing the underlined number with *three,* then *four.* Yo ho! Time to set sail!

Yo ho! We sail the sea — *(Rock body from side to side.)*
To spot a mighty whale. — *(Hold hand across top of brow.)*
Yo ho! Ahoy, there's one! — *(Hold up one finger.)*
One whale that flips its tail! — *(Flip hand up and down.)*

Yo ho! We sail the sea — *(Rock body from side to side.)*
To spot a mighty whale. — *(Hold hand across top of brow.)*
Yo ho! Ahoy, there are [two]! — *(Hold up two fingers.)*
[Two] whales that flip their tails! — *(Flip hands up and down.)*

Wonderful Water Whales

Each of your students will enjoy making this wonderful whale for some water-play fun and for a keepsake as well. For every two students in your class, cut a four-inch Styrofoam® egg in half lengthwise. Have each child paint his egg half with black, blue, or gray craft paint to represent a whale's body. Set the painted whale aside to dry overnight. Duplicate the large whale-base pattern on page 96 on a sheet of tagboard; then cut out the pattern for use as a template. For each child trace the template onto a sheet of craft foam in the desired whale color. Then help the child cut out the whale base along the outline. Have him glue the flat, broad end of his egg half to the rounded end of the whale base. Then encourage the student to glue wiggle eyes onto the sides of his whale's head and to poke a pipe-cleaner spout into the top of its head. After the glue dries, invite small groups of youngsters to take turns playing with their whales at the water table.

Magnificent Manipulatives

Use more models of these magnificent mammals to provide students with practice in sorting, counting, and patterning. To prepare, purchase a supply of four-inch and two-inch Styrofoam® eggs; then duplicate the large and small whale-base patterns (page 96) on a sheet of tagboard. Cut out each pattern to use as a template. Then have youngsters help create a supply of large and small whale models as described in "Wonderful Water Whales" in each of four different colors—black, blue, gray, and white. If desired, substitute felt for the craft foam used as the whale base. Invite children to use the whale models in some of these suggested activities:

- Glue a whale of each color to the top of a sheet of same-colored construction paper. Invite a child to sort the remaining whales by color, placing each on the appropriate color of construction paper.

- Cut nine blue, construction-paper strips to resemble waves. Program each strip with a different numeral from 1 to 9. Have a youngster place the appropriate number of whales on each wave strip.

- Glue several whales to form a pattern on each of several different blue construction-paper wave strips. Encourage a student to place whales on the strip to continue the pattern.

Cetacean Stories To Share

Dive into these whale tales and related activities with your students. Then, for each child, duplicate a copy of the bookmark on page 96 on construction paper. Send the bookmark home with each child to encourage him and his family to enjoy a sampling of the sea of cetacean stories available from libraries, bookstores, and publishers.

Baby Beluga
by Raffi
(Crown Publishers, Inc.)

This playful story captures the fun-loving and peaceful nature of the white—or beluga—whale. Prior to sharing the story, inflate a classroom supply of white balloons, tying the end of each so that the balloon resembles a whale's body and tail. Draw both an eye and a mouth on opposite sides of the broad end of the balloon-whale. Then tape a white construction-paper flipper to each side of the whale's body. Read the story aloud, giving students ample opportunity to enjoy the bright illustrations. Then give each child a balloon-whale and play the song by the same name and author from the album *Baby Beluga* (Troubadour Records). While the song is playing, invite each youngster to move himself and his whale through an imaginary deep blue sea.
(*Please note: Uninflated balloons create a choking hazard for small children. Keep them out of the reach of youngsters.)

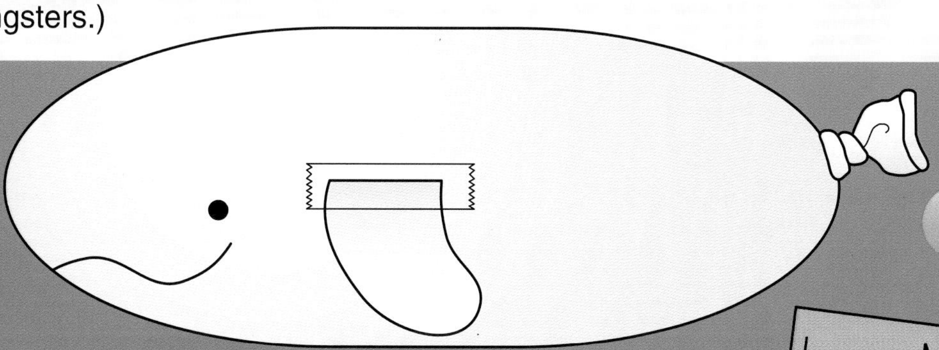

Winter Whale
by Joanne Ryder
(Mulberry Books)

The rain is falling steadily and your imagination begins to swim and take a dive into a fascinating underwater world where sea creatures grace the water and waves—and you're the giant among them all! Create this imaginary scene for youngsters prior to reading this story about the huge and powerful humpback whale. Then encourage students to imagine themselves as whales while they listen to the book being read aloud. Afterward invite each student to help illustrate a class book about his imaginary experience. Give each student a large sheet of white construction paper. Ask her to draw a picture of a whale on her paper; then have her dictate her favorite experience as an imaginary whale. Write her dictation on her paper. Stack the completed pages between two construction-paper covers and bind the book on the left edge. Write the title "My Day As A Whale" on the front cover; then place the book in the reading center for youngsters to enjoy.

Whale Head And Tail Book Covers

Use with "A Whale Of A Book!" on page 87.

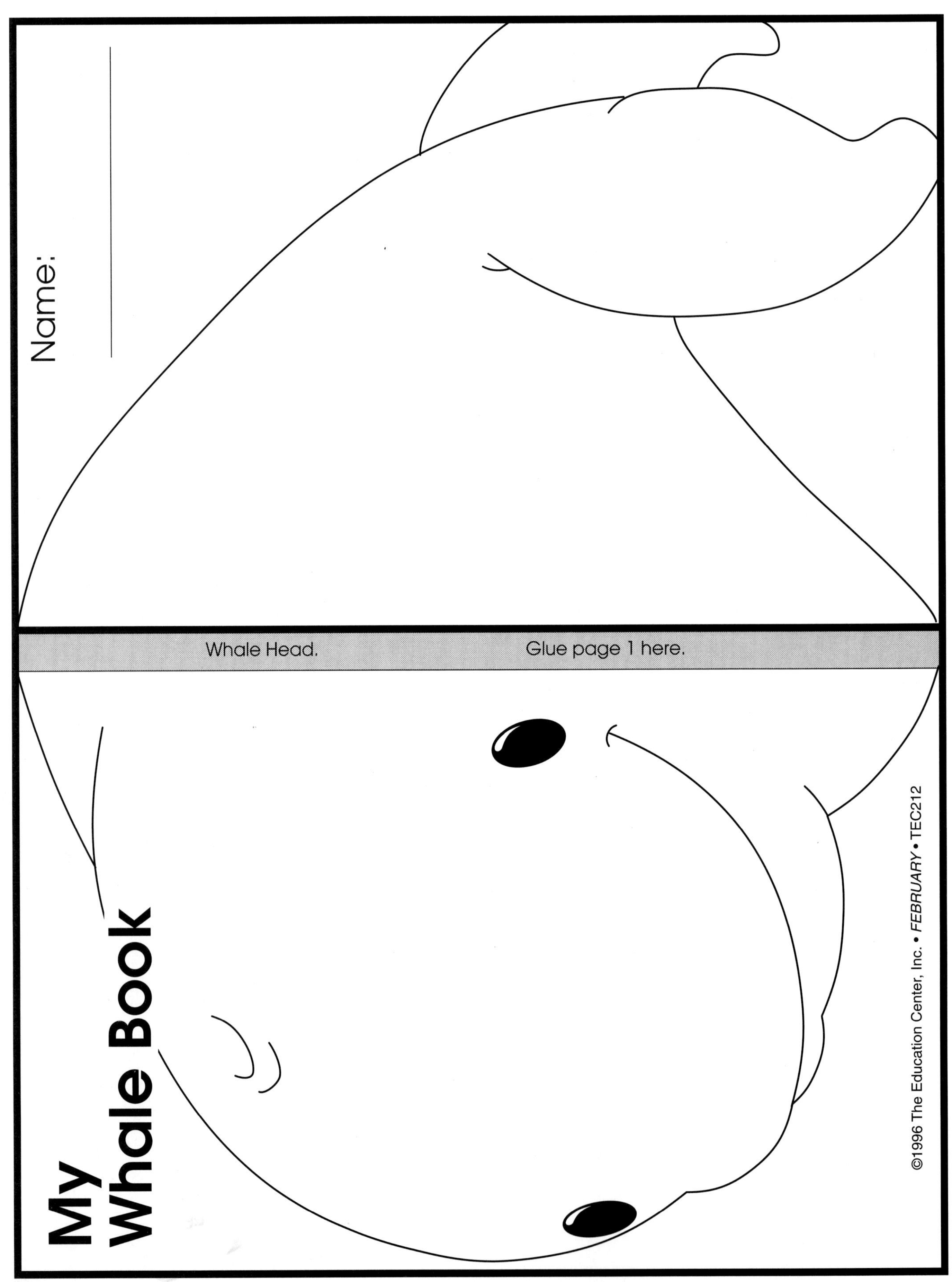

Whale Flannelboard Figures

Use with "Those Cetacean Sensations!" on page 86,
"All Kinds Of Whales" on page 87, and
"A Whopper Of A Whale!" and
"A Salty Whale Chanty" on page 89.

Beluga Whale

Orca Whale

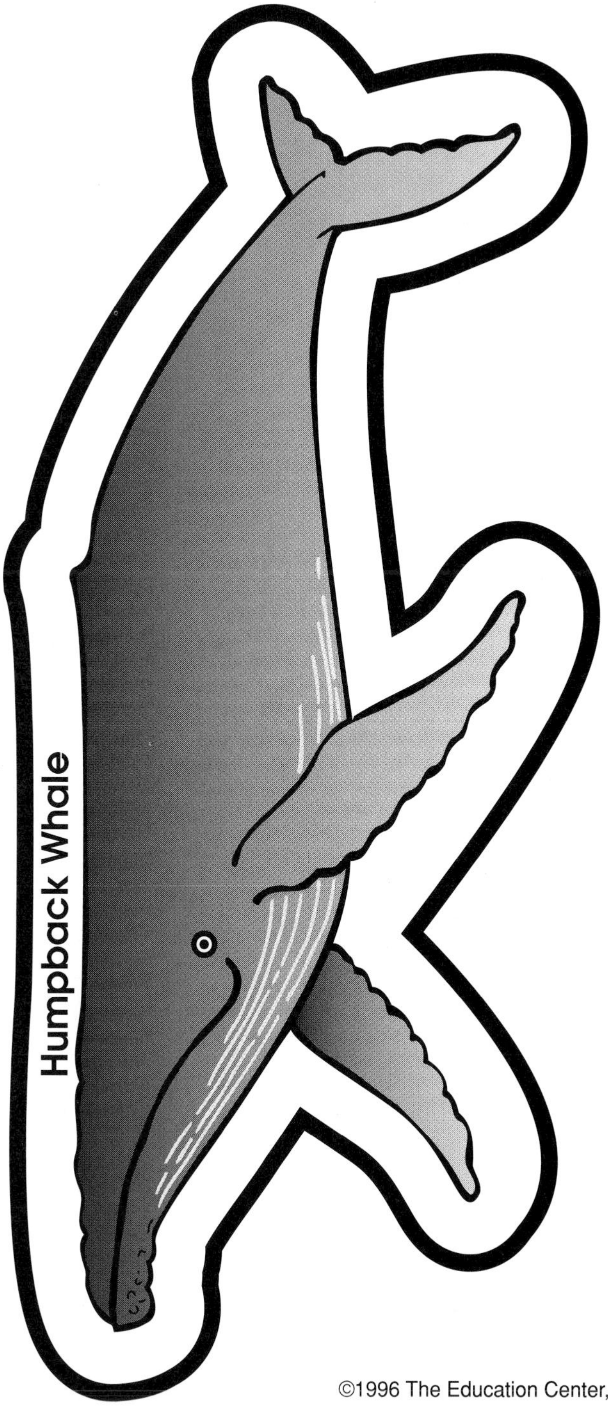

Humpback Whale

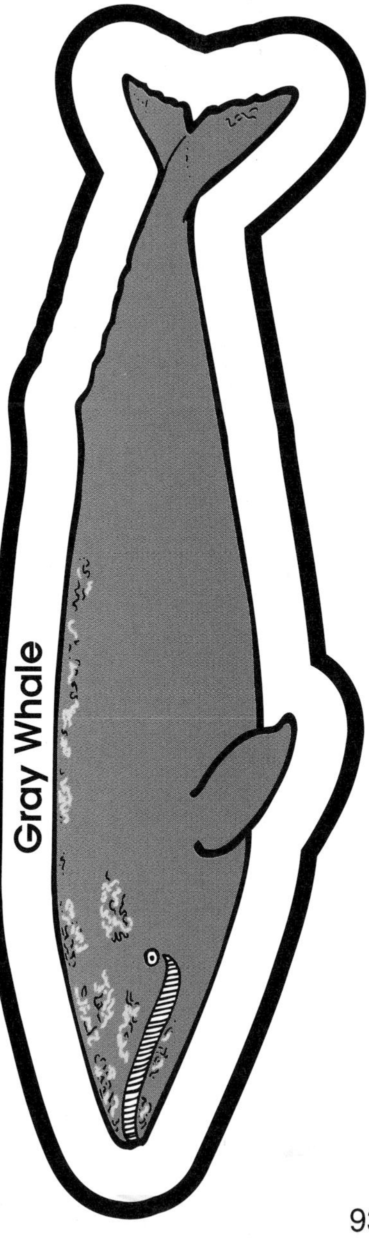

Gray Whale

Book Pages

Use with "A Whale Of A Book!" on page 87.

Glue page 3 here.

A whale breathes through a blowhole on the top of its head.

2

A whale lives in the ocean.

1

Use with "A Whale Of A Book!" on page 87.

Whale-Base Patterns

Use with "Wonderful Water Whales" and "Magnificent Manipulatives" on page 90.

Wonderful Whale Tales

Get your flippers on some good whale tales from a library, bookstore, or publisher and have a whale of a good time reading with your child.

Going On A Whale Watch
Written by Bruce McMillan
Published by Scholastic Inc.

Humphrey, The Lost Whale
Written by Wendy Tokuda and Richard Hall
Published by Heian International, Inc.

The Whale's Song
Written by Dyan Sheldon
Published by Dial Books For Young Readers

Ibis: A True Whale Story
Written by John Himmelman
Published by Scholastic Inc.

Baby Whales Drink Milk
Written by Barbara Juster Esbensen
Published by HarperCollins Publishers

Whale Bookmark

Use with "Cetacean Stories To Share" on page 91.